D0896901

GEOMETRY

Units

6 | 7 | 8

STUDENT WORKBOOK

Book 3

ISBN 978-1-5249-9134-0

AGA1.0

Related Events

Conditional Probability

Kendall Hunt

GEOMETRY

Unit 6

STUDENT WORKBOOK

Book 3

Lesson 1: Rigid Transformations in the Plane

- Let's try transformations with coordinates.

1.1: Traversing the Plane

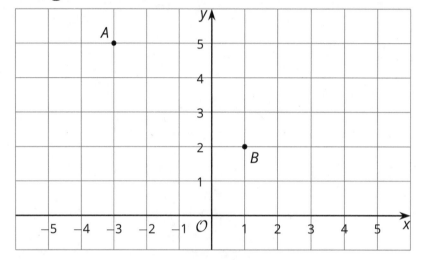

1. How far is point A from point B?

2. What transformations will take point A to point B?

1.2: Transforming with Coordinates

First, predict where each transformation will land. Next, carry out the transformation.

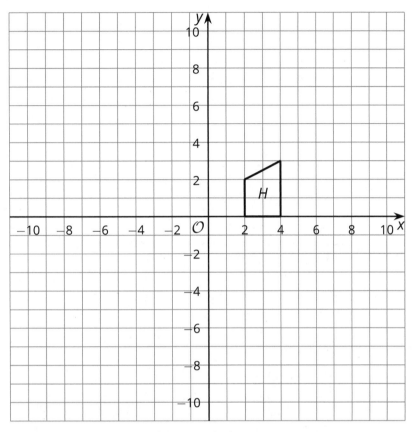

1. Rotate Figure H clockwise using center $(2, 0)$ by 90 degrees.
   Translate the image by the directed line segment from $(2, 0)$ to $(3, -4)$.
   Label the result R.

2. Reflect Figure H across the y-axis.
   Rotate the image counterclockwise using center $(0, 0)$ by 90 degrees.
   Label the result L.

1.3: Congruent by Coordinates

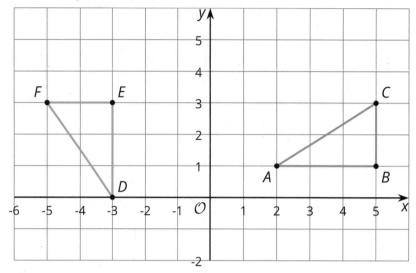

1. Calculate the length of each side in triangles ABC and DEF.

2. Calculate the measure of each angle in triangles ABC and DEF.

3. The triangles are congruent. How do you know this is true?

4. Because the triangles are congruent, there must be a sequence of rigid motions that takes one to the other. Find a sequence of rigid motions that takes triangle ABC to triangle DEF.

Are you ready for more?

What single transformation would take triangle ABC to triangle DEF?

Lesson 1 Summary

The triangles shown here look like they might be congruent. Since we know the coordinates of all the vertices, we can compare lengths using the Pythagorean Theorem. The length of segment AB is $\sqrt{13}$ units because the segment is the hypotenuse of a right triangle with vertical side length 3 units and horizontal side length 2 units. The length of segment DE is $\sqrt{13}$ units as well, because this segment is also the hypotenuse of a right triangle with leg lengths 3 and 2 units.

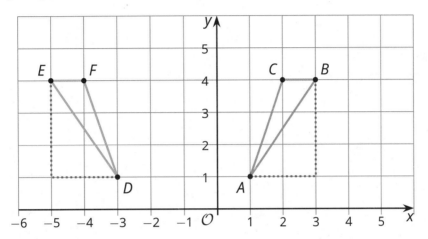

The other sides of the triangles are congruent as well: The lengths of segments BC and FE are 1 unit each, and the lengths of segments AC and DF are each $\sqrt{10}$ units, because they are both hypotenuses of right triangles with leg lengths 1 and 3 units. So triangle ABC is congruent to triangle DEF by the Side-Side-Side Triangle Congruence Theorem.

Since triangle ABC is congruent to triangle DEF, there is a sequence of rigid motions that takes triangle ABC to triangle DEF. Here is one possible sequence: First, reflect triangle ABC across the y-axis. Then, translate the image by the directed line segment from $(-1, 1)$ to $(-3, 1)$.

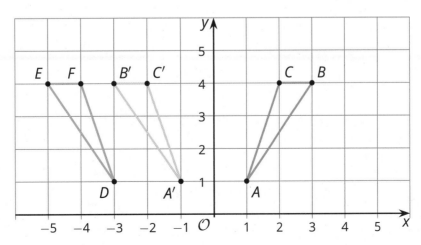

Lesson 1 Practice Problems

1. Reflect triangle ABC over the line $x = -3$.

   Translate the image by the directed line segment from $(0, 0)$ to $(4, 1)$.

   What are the coordinates of the vertices in the final image?

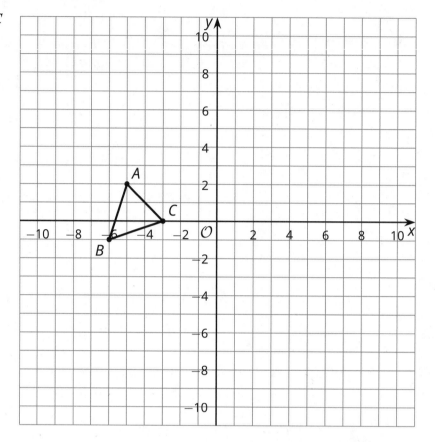

2. Three line segments form the letter N. Rotate the letter N counterclockwise around the midpoint of segment BC by 180 degrees. Describe the result.

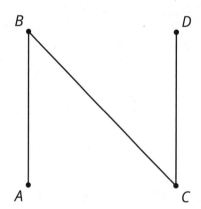

(From Unit 1, Lesson 14.)

Geometry iM KH

3. Triangle ABC has coordinates $A = (1, 3)$, $B = (2, 0)$, and $C = (4, 1)$. The image of this triangle after a sequence of transformations is triangle $A'B'C'$ where $A' = (-5, -3)$, $B' = (-4, 0)$, and $C' = (-2, -1)$.

Write a sequence of transformations that takes triangle ABC to triangle $A'B'C'$.

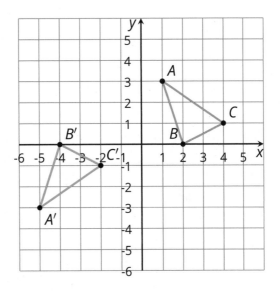

4. Prove triangle ABC is congruent to triangle DEF.

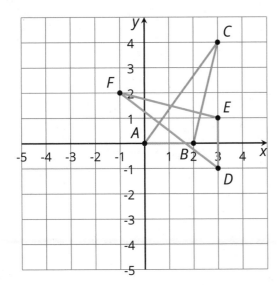

5. The density of water is 1 gram per cm^3. An object floats in water if its density is less than water's density, and it sinks if its density is greater than water's. Will a 1.17 gram diamond in the shape of a pyramid whose base has area 2 cm^2 and whose height is 0.5 centimeters sink or float? Explain your reasoning.

(From Unit 5, Lesson 17.)

6. *Technology required.* An oblique cylinder with a base of radius 2 units is shown. The top of the cylinder can be obtained by translating the base by the directed line segment AB which has length 16 units. The segment AB forms a 30° angle with the plane of the base. What is the volume of the cylinder?

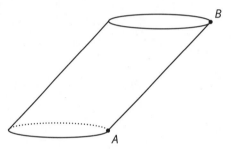

(From Unit 5, Lesson 11.)

7. This design began from the construction of an equilateral triangle. Record at least 3 rigid transformations (rotation, reflection, translation) you see in the design.

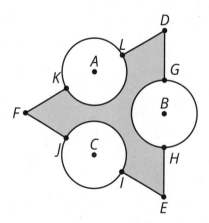

(From Unit 1, Lesson 22.)

Lesson 2: Transformations as Functions

- Let's compare transformations to functions.

2.1: Math Talk: Transforming a Point

Mentally find the coordinates of the image of A under each transformation.

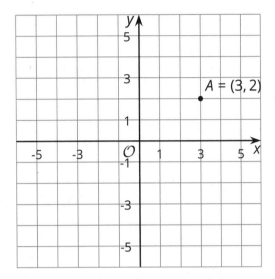

- Translate A by the directed line segment from $(0, 0)$ to $(0, 2)$.

- Translate A by the directed line segment from $(0, 0)$ to $(-4, 0)$.

- Reflect A across the x-axis.

- Rotate A 180 degrees clockwise using the origin as a center.

2.2: Inputs and Outputs

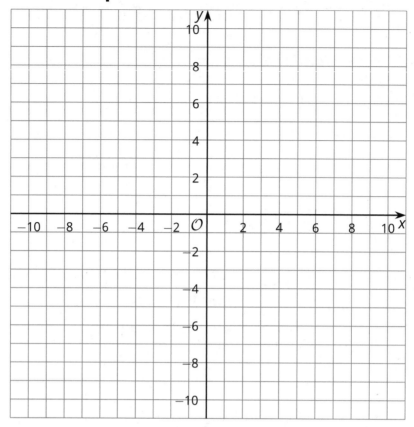

1. For each point (x, y), find its image under the transformation $(x + 12, y - 2)$.
   a. $A = (-10, 5)$

   b. $B = (-4, 9)$

   c. $C = (-2, 6)$

2. Next, sketch triangle ABC and its image on the grid. What transformation is $(x, y) \rightarrow (x + 12, y - 2)$?

3. For each point (x, y) in the table, find $(2x, 2y)$.

(x, y)	$(2x, 2y)$
(-1, -3)	
(-1, 1)	
(5, 1)	
(5, -3)	

4. Next, sketch the original figure (the (x, y) column) and image (the $(2x, 2y)$ column). What transformation is $(x, y) \rightarrow (2x, 2y)$?

2.3: What Does it Do?

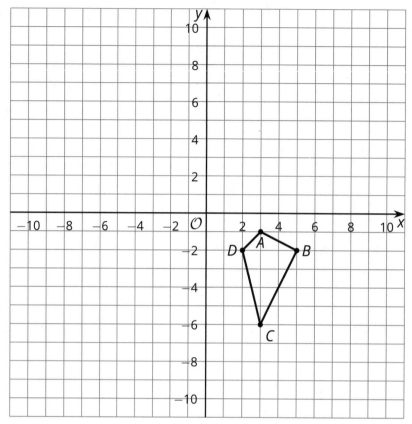

1. Here are some transformation rules. Apply each rule to quadrilateral $ABCD$ and graph the resulting image. Then describe the transformation.

   a. Label this transformation $Q: (x, y) \rightarrow (2x, y)$

   b. Label this transformation $R: (x, y) \rightarrow (x, -y)$

   c. Label this transformation $S: (x, y) \rightarrow (y, -x)$

Geometry iM KH

Are you ready for more?

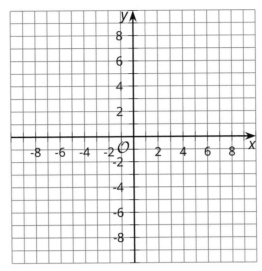

1. Plot the quadrilateral with vertices (4, -2), (8, 4), (8, -6), and (-6, -6). Label this quadrilateral A.

2. Plot the quadrilateral with vertices (-2, 4), (4, 8), (-6, 8), and (-6, -6). Label this quadrilateral A'.

3. How are the coordinates of quadrilateral A related to the coordinates of quadrilateral A'?

4. What single transformation takes quadrilateral A to quadrilateral A'?

Lesson 2 Summary

Square $ABCD$ has been translated by the directed line segment from $(-1, 1)$ to $(4, 0)$. The result is square $A'B'C'D'$.

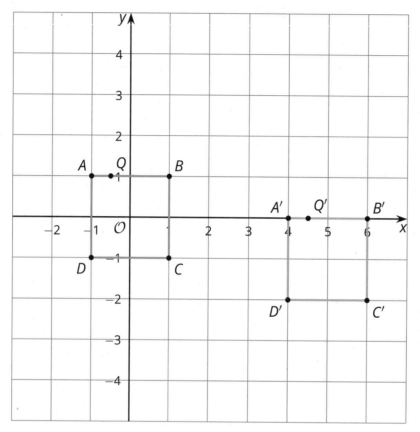

Here is a list of coordinates in the original figure and corresponding coordinates in the image. Do you see the rule for taking points in the original figure to points in the image?

original figure	image
$A = (-1, 1)$	$A' = (4, 0)$
$B = (1, 1)$	$B' = (6, 0)$
$C = (1, -1)$	$C' = (6, -2)$
$D = (-1, -1)$	$D' = (4, -2)$
$Q = (-0.5, 1)$	$Q' = (4.5, 0)$

This table looks like a table that shows corresponding inputs and outputs of a function. A transformation is a special type of function that takes points in the plane as inputs and gives other points as outputs. In this case, the function's rule is to add 5 to the x-coordinate and subtract 1 from the y-coordinate.

We write the rule this way:
$(x, y) \rightarrow (x + 5, y - 1)$.

Lesson 2 Practice Problems

1. Match each coordinate rule to a description of its resulting transformation.

   A. $(x, y) \rightarrow (x + 3, y)$

   B. $(x, y) \rightarrow (2x, 2y)$

   C. $(x, y) \rightarrow (x, y + 4)$

   D. $(x, y) \rightarrow (x, y - 4)$

   E. $(x, y) \rightarrow (x - 3, y + 4)$

   1. Translate by the directed line segment from $(0, 0)$ to $(0, 4)$.

   2. Translate by the directed line segment from $(0, 0)$ to $(3, 0)$.

   3. Dilate using the origin as the center and a scale factor of 2.

   4. Translate by the directed line segment from $(0, 0)$ to $(0, -4)$.

   5. Translate by the directed line segment from $(0, 0)$ to $(-3, 4)$.

2. a. Draw the image of triangle ABC under the transformation $(x, y) \rightarrow (x - 4, y + 1)$. Label the result T.

    b. Draw the image of triangle ABC under the transformation $(x, y) \rightarrow (-x, y)$. Label the result R.

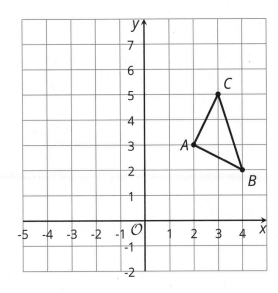

3. Here are some transformation rules. For each rule, describe whether the transformation is a rigid motion, a dilation, or neither.

    a. $(x, y) \rightarrow (x - 2, y - 3)$

    b. $(x, y) \rightarrow (2x, 3y)$

    c. $(x, y) \rightarrow (3x, 3y)$

    d. $(x, y) \rightarrow (2 - x, y)$

4. Reflect triangle ABC over the line $x = 0$. Call this new triangle $A'B'C'$. Then reflect triangle $A'B'C'$ over the line $y = 0$. Call the resulting triangle $A''B''C''$.

Which single transformation takes ABC to $A''B''C''$?

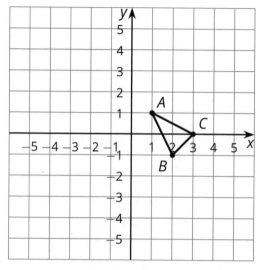

A. Translate triangle ABC by the directed line segment from $(1, 1)$ to $(-2, 1)$.

B. Reflect triangle ABC across the line $y = $ -x.

C. Rotate triangle ABC counterclockwise using the origin as the center by 180 degrees.

D. Dilate triangle ABC using the origin as the center and a scale factor of 2.

(From Unit 6, Lesson 1.)

5. Reflect triangle ABC over the line $y = 2$.

   Translate the image by the directed line segment from $(0, 0)$ to $(3, 2)$.

   What are the coordinates of the vertices in the final image?

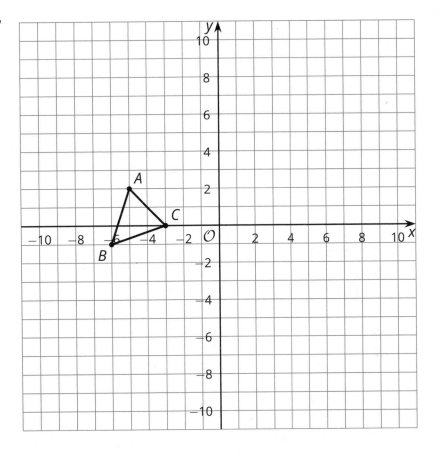

(From Unit 6, Lesson 1.)

6. The density of water is 1 gram per cm^3. An object floats in water if its density is less than water's density, and it sinks if its density is greater than water's. Will a cylindrical log with radius 0.4 meters, height 5 meters, and mass 1,950 kilograms sink or float? Explain your reasoning.

(From Unit 5, Lesson 17.)

7. These 3 congruent square pyramids can be assembled into a cube with side length 3 feet. What is the volume of each pyramid?

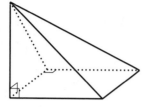 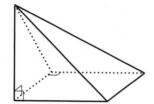 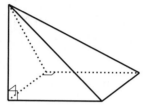

A. 1 cubic foot

B. 3 cubic feet

C. 9 cubic feet

D. 27 cubic feet

(From Unit 5, Lesson 12.)

8. Reflect square $ABCD$ across line CD. What is the ratio of the length of segment AA' to the length of segment AD? Explain or show your reasoning.

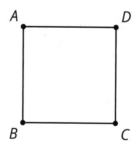

(From Unit 2, Lesson 1.)

Geometry iM KH

Lesson 3: Types of Transformations

- Let's analyze transformations that produce congruent and similar figures.

3.1: Why is it a Dilation?

Point B was transformed using the coordinate rule $(x, y) \rightarrow (3x, 3y)$.

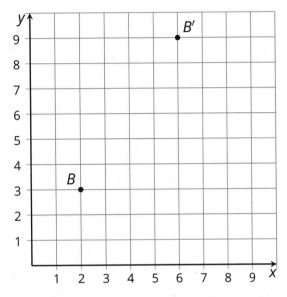

1. Add these auxiliary points and lines to create 2 right triangles: Label the origin P. Plot points $M = (2, 0)$ and $N = (6, 0)$. Draw segments PB', MB, and NB'.

2. How do triangles PMB and PNB' compare? How do you know?

3. What must be true about the ratio $PB : PB'$?

3.2: Congruent, Similar, Neither?

Match each image to its rule. Then, for each rule, decide whether it takes the original figure to a congruent figure, a similar figure, or neither. Explain or show your reasoning.

A

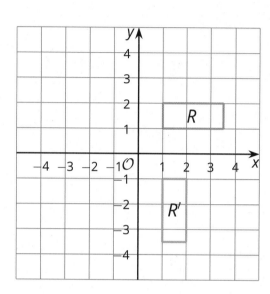

B

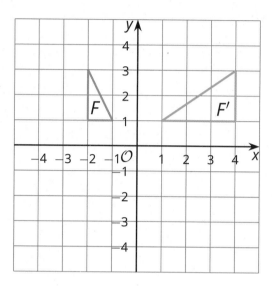

C

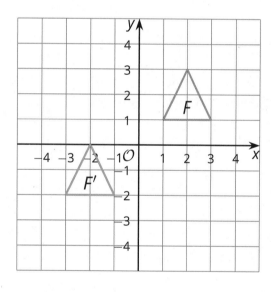

D

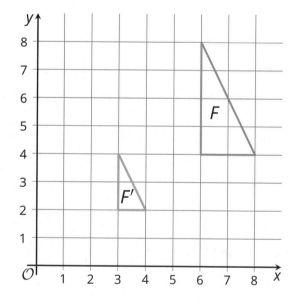

1. $(x, y) \rightarrow \left(\frac{x}{2}, \frac{y}{2} \right)$

2. $(x, y) \rightarrow (y, -x)$

3. $(x, y) \rightarrow (-3x, y)$

4. $(x, y) \rightarrow (x - 4, y - 3)$

Are you ready for more?

Here is triangle A.

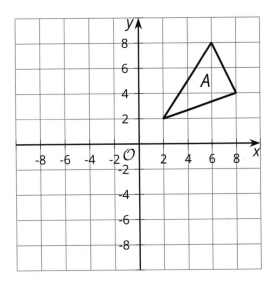

1. Reflect triangle A across the line $x = 2$.

2. Write a single rule that reflects triangle A across the line $x = 2$.

3.3: You Write the Rules

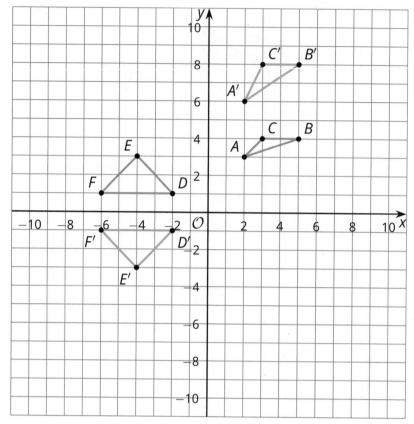

1. Write a rule that will transform triangle ABC to triangle $A'B'C'$.

2. Are ABC and $A'B'C'$ congruent? Similar? Neither? Explain how you know.

3. Write a rule that will transform triangle DEF to triangle $D'E'F'$.

4. Are DEF and $D'E'F'$ congruent? Similar? Neither? Explain how you know.

Lesson 3 Summary

Triangle ABC has been transformed in two different ways:

- $(x, y) \rightarrow (-y, x)$, resulting in triangle DEF

- $(x, y) \rightarrow (x, 3y)$, resulting in triangle XYC

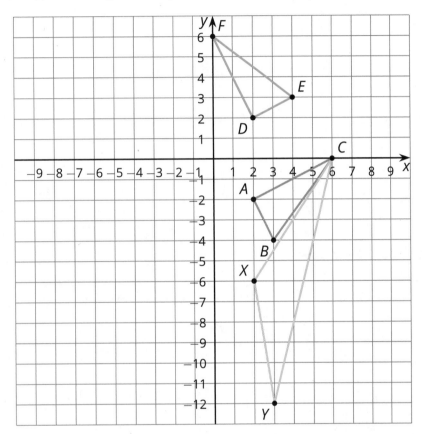

Let's analyze the effects of the first transformation. If we calculate the lengths of all the sides, we find that segments AB and DE each measure $\sqrt{5}$ units, BC and EF each measure 5 units, and AC and DF each measure $\sqrt{20}$ units. The triangles are congruent by the Side-Side-Side Triangle Congruence Theorem. That is, this transformation leaves the lengths and angles in the triangle the same—it is a rigid transformation.

Not all transformations keep lengths or angles the same. Compare triangles ABC and XYC. Angle X is larger than angle A. All of the side lengths of XYC are larger than their corresponding sides. The transformation $(x, y) \rightarrow (x, 3y)$ stretches the points on the triangle 3 times farther away from the x-axis. This is not a rigid transformation. It is also not a dilation since the corresponding angles are not congruent.

Lesson 3 Practice Problems

1. Complete the table and determine the rule for this transformation.

input	output
$(2, -3)$	$(-3, 2)$
$(4, 5)$	$(5, 4)$
$(\_\_, 4)$	$(4, 0)$
$(1, 6)$	
	$(-1, -2)$
(x, y)	

2. Write a rule that describes this transformation.

original figure	image
$(5, 1)$	$(2, -1)$
$(-3, 4)$	$(-6, -4)$
$(1, -2)$	$(-2, 2)$
$(-1, -4)$	$(-4, 4)$

3. Select **all** the transformations that produce congruent images.

   A. dilation

   B. horizontal stretch

   C. reflection

   D. rotation

   E. translation

4. Here are some transformation rules. For each transformation, first predict what the image of triangle ABC will look like. Then compute the coordinates of the image and draw it.

   a. $(x, y) \rightarrow (x - 4, y - 1)$

   b. $(x, y) \rightarrow (y, x)$

   c. $(x, y) \rightarrow (1.5x, 1.5y)$

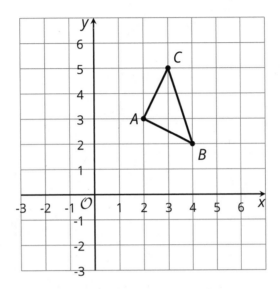

(From Unit 6, Lesson 2.)

5. A cylinder has radius 3 inches and height 5 inches. A cone has the same radius and height.

   a. Find the volume of the cylinder.

   b. Find the volume of the cone.

   c. What fraction of the cylinder's volume is the cone's volume?

(From Unit 5, Lesson 13.)

6. Reflect triangle ABC over the line $x = -2$. Call this new triangle $A'B'C'$. Then reflect triangle $A'B'C'$ over the line $x = 0$. Call the resulting triangle $A''B''C''$.

Describe a single transformation that takes ABC to $A''B''C''$.

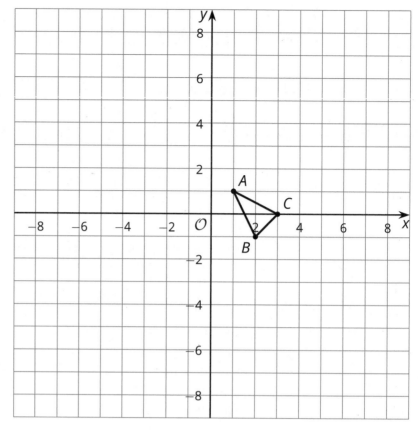

(From Unit 6, Lesson 1.)

7. In the construction, A is the center of one circle, and B is the center of the other.

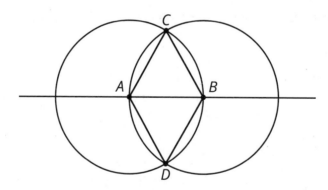

Explain why segments AC, BC, AD, BD, and AB have the same length.

(From Unit 1, Lesson 2.)

Geometry iM KH

Lesson 4: Distances and Circles

- Let's build an equation for a circle.

4.1: Going the Distance

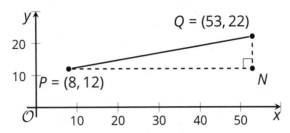

Andre says, "I know that I can find the distance between two points in the plane by drawing in a right triangle and using the Pythagorean Theorem. But I'm not sure how to find the lengths of the legs of the triangle when I can't just count the squares on the graph."

Explain to Andre how he can find the lengths of the legs in the triangle in the image. Then, calculate the distance between points P and Q.

4.2: Circling the Problem

The image shows a circle with center $(6, 10)$ and radius 17 units.

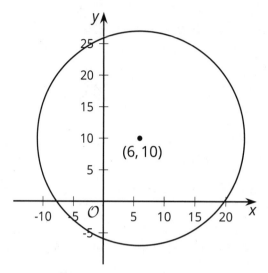

1. The point $(14, 25)$ looks like it might be on the circle. Verify if it really is on the circle. Explain or show your reasoning.

2. The point $(22, 3)$ looks like it might be on the circle. Verify if it really is on the circle. Explain or show your reasoning.

3. In general, how can you check if a particular point (x, y) is on the circle?

Are you ready for more?

The image shows segment AB and several points.

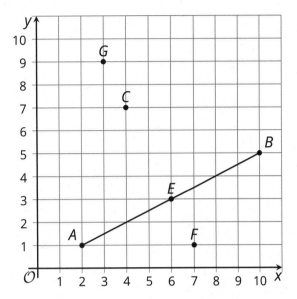

1. Calculate the distance from each point to the endpoints of segment AB.

	point A	point B
point G		
point C		
point E		
point F		

2. What do the distances tell you about points $G, E, C,$ and F?

4.3: Building an Equation for a Circle

The image shows a circle with center (-3, 6) and radius 13 units.

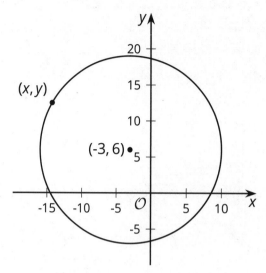

1. Write an equation that would allow you to test whether a particular point (x, y) is on the circle.

2. Use your equation to test whether $(9, 1)$ is on the circle.

3. Suppose you have a circle with center (h, k) and radius r. Write an equation that would allow you to test whether a particular point (x, y) is on the circle.

Lesson 4 Summary

The diagram shows the point $(3, 1)$, along with several points that are 5 units away from $(3, 1)$. The set of *all* points 5 units away from $(3, 1)$ is a circle with center $(3, 1)$ and radius 5.

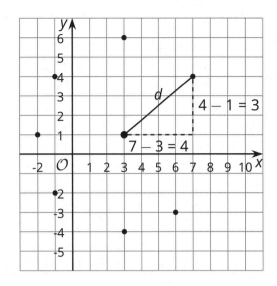

The point $(7, 4)$ appears to be on this circle. To verify, calculate the distance from $(7, 4)$ to $(3, 1)$. If this distance is 5, then the point is on the circle. Let d stand for the distance, and set up the Pythagorean Theorem: $(7 - 3)^2 + (4 - 1)^2 = d^2$. Evaluate the left hand side to find that $25 = d^2$. Now d is the positive number that squares to make 25, which means $(7, 4)$ really is 5 units away from $(3, 1)$. This point is on the circle.

The point $(8, 2)$ also looks like it could be on the circle. To find its distance from $(3, 1)$, we can do a similar calculation: $(8 - 3)^2 + (2 - 1)^2 = d^2$. Evaluating the left side, we get $26 = d^2$. This means that d must be a little more than 5. So $(8, 2)$ does not lie on the circle.

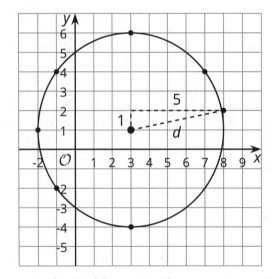

To check if any point (x, y) is on the circle, we can use the Pythagorean Theorem to see if $(x - 3)^2 + (y - 1)^2$ is equal to 5^2 or 25. Any point that satisfies this condition is on the circle, so the equation for the circle is $(x - 3)^2 + (y - 1)^2 = 25$.

By the same reasoning, a circle with center (h, k) and radius r has equation $(x - h)^2 + (y - k)^2 = r^2$.

Lesson 4 Practice Problems

1. Match each equation to its description.

   A. circle centered at $(0, -4)$ with a radius of 3

   B. circle centered at $(1, -4)$ with a radius of $\sqrt{3}$

   C. circle centered at $(1, 4)$ with a radius of $\sqrt{3}$

   D. circle centered at $(1, 0)$ with a radius of 3

   E. circle centered at $(1, -4)$ with a radius of 3

   1. $(x - 1)^2 + y^2 = 9$

   2. $x^2 + (y + 4)^2 = 9$

   3. $(x - 1)^2 + (y - 4)^2 = 3$

   4. $(x - 1)^2 + (y + 4)^2 = 9$

   5. $(x - 1)^2 + (y + 4)^2 = 3$

2. Write an equation of a circle that is centered at $(-3, 2)$ with a radius of 5.

   A. $(x - 3)^2 + (y + 2)^2 = 5$

   B. $(x + 3)^2 + (y - 2)^2 = 5$

   C. $(x - 3)^2 + (y + 2)^2 = 25$

   D. $(x + 3)^2 + (y - 2)^2 = 25$

3. a. Plot the circles $x^2 + y^2 = 4$ and $x^2 + y^2 = 1$ on the same coordinate plane.

   b. Find the image of any point on $x^2 + y^2 = 4$ under the transformation $(x, y) \rightarrow \left(\frac{1}{2}x, \frac{1}{2}y \right)$.

   c. What do you notice about $x^2 + y^2 = 4$ and $x^2 + y^2 = 1$?

4. $(x, y) \rightarrow (x - 3, 4 - y)$ is an example of a transformation called a glide reflection. Complete the table using the rule.

Does this glide reflection produce a triangle congruent to the original?

input	output
$(1, 1)$	$(-2, 3)$
$(6, 1)$	
$(3, 5)$	

(From Unit 6, Lesson 3.)

5. The triangle whose vertices are $(1, 1)$, $(5, 3)$, and $(4, 5)$ is transformed by the rule $(x, y) \rightarrow (3x, 3y)$. Is the image similar or congruent to the original figure?

    A. The image is congruent to the original triangle.

    B. The image is similar but not congruent to the original triangle.

    C. The image is neither similar nor congruent to the original triangle.

(From Unit 6, Lesson 3.)

6. Match each coordinate rule to a description of its resulting transformation.

A. $(x, y) \rightarrow (3x, 3y)$

B. $(x, y) \rightarrow (x - 3, y - 3)$

C. $(x, y) \rightarrow (x + 3, y + 3)$

D. $(x, y) \rightarrow (x - 3, y)$

E. $(x, y) \rightarrow (x + 3, y)$

F. $(x, y) \rightarrow (x, y - 3)$

G. $(x, y) \rightarrow (x, y + 3)$

1. Translate along the directed line segment from $(0, 0)$ to (-3, 0).

2. Translate along the directed line segment from $(0, 0)$ to (0, -3).

3. Translate along the directed line segment from $(0, 0)$ to (3, 0).

4. Translate along the directed line segment from $(0, 0)$ to (0, 3).

5. Translate along the directed line segment from $(0, 0)$ to (3, 3).

6. Translate along the directed line segment from $(0, 0)$ to (-3, -3).

7. Dilate using the origin as the center and a scale factor of 3.

(From Unit 6, Lesson 2.)

7. A cone-shaped container is oriented with its circular base on the top and its apex at the bottom. It has a radius of 18 inches and a height of 6 inches. The cone starts filling up with water. What fraction of the volume of the cone is filled when the water reaches a height of 2 inches?

A. $\frac{1}{729}$

B. $\frac{1}{27}$

C. $\frac{1}{9}$

D. $\frac{1}{3}$

(From Unit 5, Lesson 14.)

Geometry iM KH

Lesson 5: Squares and Circles

- Let's see how the distributive property can relate to equations of circles.

5.1: Math Talk: Distribution

Distribute each expression mentally.

$5(x + 3)$

$x(x - 3)$

$(x + 4)(x + 2)$

$(x - 5)(x - 5)$

5.2: Perfectly Square

1. Apply the distributive property to each expression.

    a. $(x - 7)(x - 7)$

    b. $(x + 4)^2$

    c. $(x - 10)^2$

    d. $(x + 1)^2$

2. Look at your results. Each of these expressions is called a *perfect square trinomial*. Why?

3. Which of these expressions are perfect square trinomials? If you get stuck, look for patterns in your earlier work.

    a. $x^2 - 6x + 9$

    b. $x^2 + 10x + 20$

    c. $x^2 + 18x + 81$

    d. $x^2 - 2x + 1$

    e. $x^2 + 4x + 16$

4. Rewrite the perfect square trinomials you identified as squared binomials.

5.3: Back and Forth

1. Here is the equation of a circle: $(x - 2)^2 + (y + 7)^2 = 10^2$

    a. What are the center and radius of the circle?

    b. Apply the distributive property to the squared binomials and rearrange the equation so that one side is 0. This is the form in which many circle equations are written.

2. This equation looks different, but also represents a circle:
   $$x^2 + 6x + 9 + y^2 - 10y + 25 = 64$$

    a. How can you rewrite this equation to find the center and radius of the circle?

    b. What are the center and radius of the circle?

Are you ready for more?

In three-dimensional space, there are 3 coordinate axes, called the x-axis, the y-axis, and the z-axis. Write an equation for a sphere with center (a, b, c) and radius r.

Lesson 5 Summary

Suppose we square several binomials, or expressions that contain 2 terms. We get trinomials, or expressions that contain 3 terms. Does any pattern emerge in the results?

$$(x + 6)^2 = x^2 + 12x + 36$$

$$(x - 8)^2 = x^2 - 16x + 64$$

$$(x + 5)^2 = x^2 + 10x + 25$$

Each of the expressions on the right are called perfect square trinomials because they are the result of multiplying an expression by itself. There is a pattern in the results: When the coefficient of x^2 in a trinomial is 1, if the constant term is the square of half the coefficient of x, then the expression is a perfect square trinomial.

For example, $x^2 - 14x + 49$ is a perfect square trinomial because the constant term, 49, can be rewritten as $(-7)^2$, and half of -14 is -7. This expression can be rewritten as a squared binomial: $(x - 7)^2$.

Two squared binomials show up in the equation for circles: $(x - h)^2 + (y - k)^2 = r^2$. Equations for circles are sometimes written in different forms, but we can rearrange them to help find the center and radius of the circle. For example, suppose the equation of a circle is written like this:

$$x^2 - 22x + 121 + y^2 + 2y + 1 = 225$$

We can't immediately identify the center and radius of the circle. However, if we rewrite the two perfect square trinomials as squared binomials and rewrite the right side in the form r^2, the center and radius will be easier to recognize.

The first 3 terms on the left side, $x^2 - 22x + 121$, can be rewritten as $(x - 11)^2$. The remaining terms, $y^2 + 2y + 1$, can be rewritten as $(y + 1)^2$. The right side, 225, can be rewritten as 15^2. Let's put it all together.

$$(x - 11)^2 + (y + 1)^2 = 15^2$$

Now we can see that the center of the circle is $(11, -1)$ and the circle's radius measures 15 units.

Lesson 5 Practice Problems

1. Match each quadratic expression with an equivalent expression in factored form.

A. $x^2 + 6x$

B. $x^2 + 6x + 5$

C. $x^2 + 6x - 7$

D. $x^2 + 6x + 8$

E. $x^2 + 6x + 9$

1. $(x + 7)(x - 1)$

2. $(x + 5)(x + 1)$

3. $(x + 4)(x + 2)$

4. $(x + 3)(x + 3)$

5. $x(x + 6)$

2. An equation of a circle is $x^2 - 8x + 16 + y^2 + 10y + 25 = 81$.

a. What is the radius of the circle?

b. What is the center of the circle?

3. Write 3 perfect square trinomials. Then rewrite them as squared binomials.

4. Write an equation of the circle that has a diameter with endpoints $(12, 3)$ and $(-18, 3)$.

(From Unit 6, Lesson 4.)

5. a. Graph the circle
    $(x - 2)^2 + (y - 1)^2 = 25$.

    b. For each point, determine if it is on the circle. If not, decide whether it is inside the circle or outside of the circle.

    i. $(4, 0)$

    ii. $(-3, 3)$

    iii. $(-2, -2)$

    c. How can you use distance calculations to decide if a point is inside, on, or outside a circle?

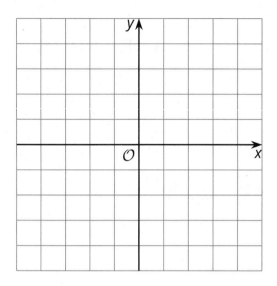

(From Unit 6, Lesson 4.)

6. The triangle whose vertices are $(2, 5), (3, 1)$, and $(4, 2)$ is transformed by the rule $(x, y) \rightarrow (x - 2, y + 4)$. Is the image similar or congruent to the original figure?

    A. The image is congruent to the original triangle.

    B. The image is similar but not congruent to the original triangle.

    C. The image is neither similar nor congruent to the original triangle.

(From Unit 6, Lesson 3.)

7. *Technology required.* A triangular prism has height 6 units. The base of the prism is shown in the image. What is the volume of the prism? Round your answer to the nearest tenth.

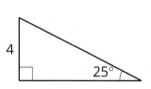

(From Unit 5, Lesson 15.)

Lesson 6: Completing the Square

- Let's rewrite equations to find the center and radius of a circle.

6.1: Fill in the Box

For each expression, what value would need to be in the box in order for the expression to be a perfect square trinomial?

1. $x^2 + 10x + \boxed{}$

2. $x^2 - 16x + \boxed{}$

3. $x^2 + 40x + \boxed{}$

4. $x^2 + 5x + \boxed{}$

6.2: Complete the Process

Here is the equation of a circle: $x^2 + y^2 - 6x - 20y + 105 = 0$

Elena wants to find the center and radius of the circle. Here is what she's done so far.

Step 1: $x^2 - 6x + y^2 - 20y = \text{-}105$

Step 2: $x^2 - 6x + 9 + y^2 - 20y + 100 = \text{-}105 + 9 + 100$

Step 3: $x^2 - 6x + 9 + y^2 - 20y + 100 = 4$

1. What did Elena do in the first step?

2. Why did Elena add 9 and 100 to the *left* side of the equation in Step 2?

3. Why did Elena add 9 and 100 to the *right* side of the equation in Step 2?

4. What should Elena do next?

5. What are the center and radius of this circle?

6. Draw a graph of the circle.

6.3: Your Turn

Here is the equation of a circle: $x^2 + y^2 - 2x + 4y - 4 = 0$

1. Find the center and radius of the circle. Explain or show your reasoning.

2. Draw a graph of the circle.

Are you ready for more?

Triangulation is a process of using 3 distances from known landmarks to locate an exact position. Find a point that is located 5 units from the point $(3, 4)$, 13 units from the point $(11, -4)$, and 17 units from the point $(21, 16)$. Use the coordinate grid if it's helpful.

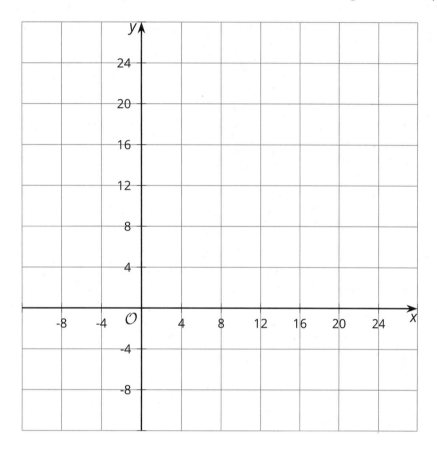

Lesson 6 Summary

Here is an equation for a circle: $x^2 + y^2 - 4x + 6y - 3 = 0$. If we want to find the center and radius of the circle, we can rewrite the equation in the form $(x - h)^2 + (y - k)^2 = r^2$.

Start by rearranging the terms in the equation to make it easier to work with. Group terms that include the same variable and move the -3 to the right side of the equation.

$$x^2 - 4x + y^2 + 6y = 3$$

We want the left side to include 2 perfect square trinomials—then, those trinomials can be rewritten in factored form to get the equation in the form we need. To create perfect square trinomials, we can add values to the left side. We'll keep the equation balanced by adding those same values to the other side.

$$x^2 - 4x + \square + y^2 + 6y + \square = 3 + \square + \square$$

For the expression $x^2 - 4x$, we need to add 4 to get a perfect square trinomial. For the expression $y^2 + 6y$, we need to add 9. Add these values to *both* sides of the equation. Then, combine the numbers on the right side.

$$x^2 - 4x + 4 + y^2 + 6y + 9 = 3 + 4 + 9$$

$$x^2 - 4x + 4 + y^2 + 6y + 9 = 16$$

Now rewrite the perfect square trinomials as squared binomials, and write the 16 in the form r^2.

$$(x - 2)^2 + (y + 3)^2 = 4^2$$

The circle has center (2, -3) and radius 4 units.

Lesson 6 Practice Problems

1. Suppose a classmate missed the lessons on completing the square to find the center and radius of a circle. Explain the process to them. If it helps, use a problem you've already done as an example.

2. Match each expression with the value needed in the box in order for the expression to be a perfect square trinomial.

   A. $x^2 - 8x + \square$

   B. $x^2 + 20x + \square$

   C. $x^2 - 16x + \square$

   D. $x^2 + 9x + \square$

   1. 16

   2. 20.25

   3. 64

   4. 100

3. Find the center and radius of the circle represented by the equation $x^2 + y^2 + 4x - 10y + 20 = 0$.

4. Select **all** the expressions that can be factored into a squared binomial.

   A. $y^2 + 2y + 1$

   B. $w^2 + 5w + \frac{25}{4}$

   C. $y^2 - 10y + 5$

   D. $x^2 - 10x + 25$

   E. $x^2 + 10x + 25$

   F. $w^2 + 20w + 40$

   (From Unit 6, Lesson 5.)

5. An equation of a circle is given by $(x + 3)^2 + (y - 9)^2 = 5^2$. Apply the distributive property to the squared binomials and rearrange the equation so that one side is 0.

   (From Unit 6, Lesson 5.)

6. a. Graph the circle
    $(x + 1)^2 + (y - 3)^2 = 16$.

    b. Find the distance from the center of
    the circle to each point on the list.
      i. $(2, 1)$

      ii. $(4, 1)$

      iii. $(3, 3)$

    c. What do these distances tell you
    about whether each point is inside,
    on, or outside the circle?

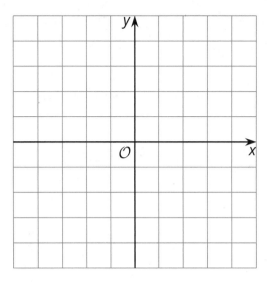

(From Unit 6, Lesson 4.)

7. The triangle whose vertices are $(3, -1), (2, 4)$, and $(5, 1)$ is transformed by the rule
   $(x, y) \rightarrow (2x, 5y)$. Is the image similar or congruent to the original figure?

    A. The image is congruent to the original triangle.

    B. The image is similar but not congruent to the original triangle.

    C. The image is neither similar nor congruent to the original triangle.

    (From Unit 6, Lesson 3.)

8. A cube has side length 3 inches. A sphere has a radius of 3 inches.

    a. Before doing any calculations, predict which solid has greater surface area to
    volume ratio.

    b. Calculate the surface area, volume, and surface area to volume ratio for each
    solid.

    (From Unit 5, Lesson 16.)

Lesson 7: Distances and Parabolas

- Let's analyze the set of points that are the same distance from a given point and a given line.

7.1: Notice and Wonder: Distances

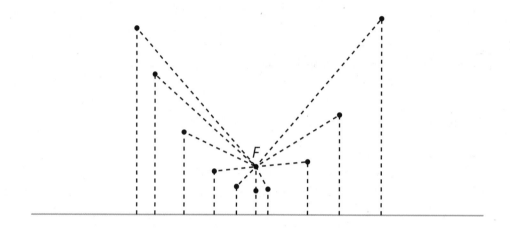

What do you notice? What do you wonder?

7.2: Into Focus

Here are several images of **parabolas**.

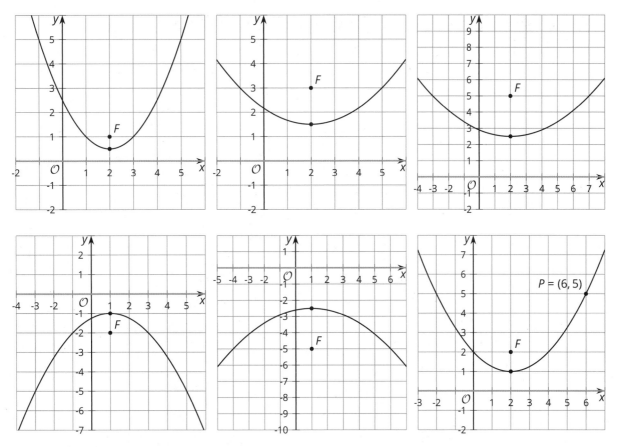

Look at the **focus** and **directrix** of each parabola. In each case, the directrix is the x-axis.

1. How does the distance between the focus and the directrix affect the shape of the parabola?

2. What seems to need to be true in order for the parabola to open downward (that is, to be shaped like a hill instead of a valley)?

3. The vertex of the parabola is the lowest point on the curve if it opens upward, or the highest if it opens downward. Where is the vertex located in relationship to the focus and the directrix?

4. In the final image, the directrix is on the x-axis and the focus is the point $(2, 2)$. Point P on the parabola is plotted.

    a. What is the distance between point P and the directrix?

    b. What does this tell you about the distance between P and F?

7.3: On Point

The image shows a parabola with focus $(6, 4)$ and directrix $y = 0$ (the x-axis).

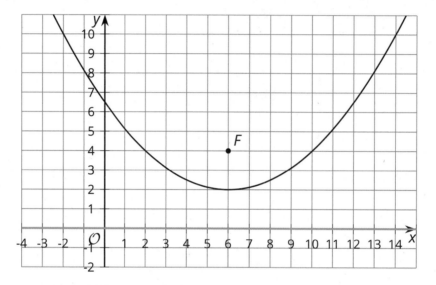

1. The point $(11, 5)$ looks like it might be on the parabola. Determine if it really is on the parabola. Explain or show your reasoning.

2. The point $(14, 10)$ looks like it might be on the parabola. Determine if it really is on the parabola. Explain or show your reasoning.

3. In general, how can you determine if a particular point (x, y) is on the parabola?

Are you ready for more?

The image shows a parabola with directrix $y = 0$ and focus at $F = (2, 5)$.

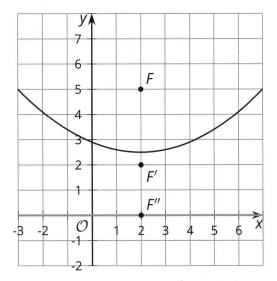

Imagine you moved the focus from F to $F' = (2, 2)$.

1. Sketch the new parabola.

2. How does decreasing the distance between the focus and the directrix change the shape of the parabola?

3. Suppose the focus were at F'', on the directrix. What would happen?

Lesson 7 Summary

The diagram shows several points that are the same distance from the point $(2, 1)$ as they are from the line $y = -3$. (Distance is measured from each point to the line along a segment perpendicular to the line.) The set of *all* points that are the same distance from a given point and a given line form a **parabola**. The given point is called the parabola's **focus** and the line is called its **directrix**.

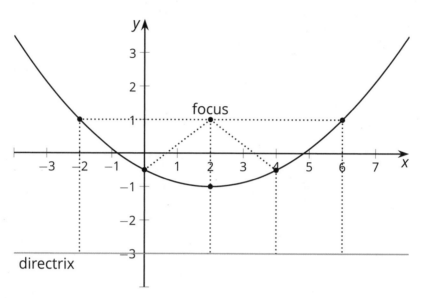

We can use this definition to test if points are on a parabola. The image shows the parabola with focus $(2, 3)$ and directrix $y = 1$. The point $(-2, 6)$ appears to be on the parabola. Counting downwards, the distance between $(-2, 6)$ and the directrix is 5 units.

Now use the Pythagorean Theorem to find the distance d between $(-2, 6)$ and the focus, $(2, 3)$. Imagine drawing a right triangle whose hypotenuse is the segment connecting $(-2, 6)$ and $(2, 3)$. The lengths of the triangle's legs can be found by subtracting the corresponding coordinates of the points.

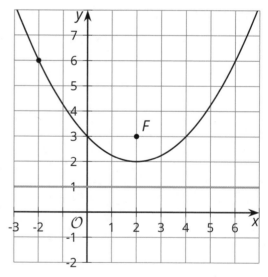

Use those lengths in the Pythagorean Theorem to get $(-2 - 2)^2 + (6 - 3)^2 = d^2$. Evaluate the left side of the equation to find that $25 = d^2$. The distance, then, is 5 units because 5 is the positive number that squares to make 25. Now we know the point $(-2, 6)$ really is on the parabola, because it's 5 units away from both the focus and the directrix.

Glossary

- directrix
- focus
- parabola

Lesson 7 Practice Problems

1. The point $(6, y)$ is the same distance from $(4, 1)$ as it is from the x-axis. What is the value of y?

2. A parabola is defined as the set of points the same distance from $(6, 2)$ and the line $y = 4$. Select **all** points that are on this parabola.

   A. $(1, -2)$

   B. $(2, -1)$

   C. $(6, 2)$

   D. $(7, 3)$

   E. $(8, 2)$

3. Compare and contrast the parabolas with these definitions.

   ○ parabola A: points that are the same distance from $(0, 4)$ and the x-axis

   ○ parabola B: points that are the same distance from $(0, -6)$ and the x-axis

4. Find the center and radius of the circle represented by the equation $x^2 + y^2 - 8y + 5 = 0$.

(From Unit 6, Lesson 6.)

5. Match each expression with the value needed in the box in order for the expression to be a perfect square trinomial.

A. $x^2 + 14x + \square$

B. $x^2 - \frac{1}{2}x + \square$

C. $c^2 - 10c + \square$

D. $z^2 + z + \square$

1. $\frac{1}{16}$

2. 49

3. 25

4. $\frac{1}{4}$

(From Unit 6, Lesson 6.)

6. Write each expression as the square of a binomial.

a. $x^2 - 12x + 36$

b. $y^2 + 8y + 16$

c. $w^2 - 16w + 64$

(From Unit 6, Lesson 5.)

7. Write an equation of a circle that is centered at (1, -4) with a radius of 10.

(From Unit 6, Lesson 4.)

8. The density of water is 1 gram per cm^3. An object floats in water if its density is less than water's density, and it sinks if its density is greater than water's. Will a solid bar of soap shaped like a rectangular prism with mass 1.048 kilograms and dimensions 5.6 centimeters, 13 centimeters, and 16 centimeters float or sink? Explain your reasoning.

(From Unit 5, Lesson 17.)

9. Jada has this idea for bisecting angle ABC. First she draws a circle with center B through A. Then she constructs the perpendicular bisector of AD.

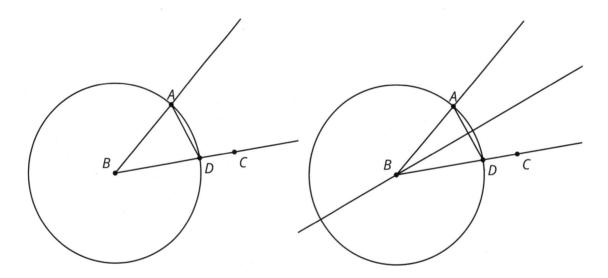

Does Jada's construction work? Explain your reasoning. You may assume that the perpendicular bisector of line segment AD is the set of points equidistant from A and D.

(From Unit 1, Lesson 5.)

Lesson 8: Equations and Graphs

- Let's write an equation for a parabola.

8.1: Focus on Distance

The image shows a parabola with focus $(-2, 2)$ and directrix $y = 0$ (the x-axis). Points A, B, and C are on the parabola.

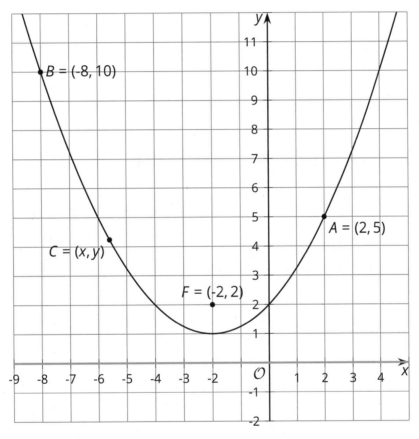

Without using the Pythagorean Theorem, find the distance from each plotted point to the parabola's focus. Explain your reasoning.

8.2: Building an Equation for a Parabola

The image shows a parabola with focus $(3, 2)$ and directrix $y = 0$ (the x-axis).

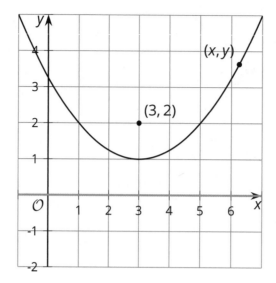

1. Write an equation that would allow you to test whether a particular point (x, y) is on the parabola.

2. The equation you wrote defines the parabola, but it's not in a very easy-to-read form. Rewrite the equation to be in vertex form: $y = a(x - h)^2 + k$, where (h, k) is the vertex.

8.3: Card Sort: Parabolas

Your teacher will give you a set of cards with graphs and equations of parabolas. Match each graph with the equation that represents it.

Are you ready for more?

In this section, you have examined points that are equidistant from a given point and a given line. Now consider a set of points that are half as far from a point as they are from a line.

1. Write an equation that describes the set of all points that are $\frac{1}{2}$ as far from the point $(5, 3)$ as they are from the x-axis.

2. Use technology to graph your equation. Sketch the graph and describe what it looks like.

Lesson 8 Summary

The parabola in the image consists of all the points that are the same distance from the point $(1, 4)$ as they are from the line $y = 0$. Suppose we want to write an equation for the parabola—that is, an equation that says a given point (x, y) is on the curve. We can draw a right triangle whose hypotenuse is the distance between point (x, y) and the focus, $(1, 4)$.

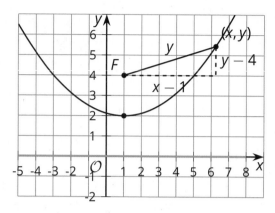

The distance from (x, y) to the directrix, or the line $y = 0$, is y units. By definition, the distance from (x, y) to the focus must be equal to the distance from the point to the directrix. So, the distance from (x, y) to the focus can be labeled with y. To find the lengths of the legs of the right triangle, subtract the corresponding coordinates of the point (x, y) and the focus, $(1, 4)$. Substitute the expressions for the side lengths into the Pythagorean Theorem to get an equation defining the parabola.

$$(x - 1)^2 + (y - 4)^2 = y^2$$

To get the equation looking more familiar, rewrite it in vertex form, or $y = a(x - h)^2 + k$ where (h, k) is the vertex.

$$(x - 1)^2 + (y - 4)^2 = y^2$$

$$(x - 1)^2 + y^2 - 8y + 16 = y^2$$

$$(x - 1)^2 - 8y + 16 = 0$$

$$-8y = -(x - 1)^2 - 16$$

$$y = \tfrac{1}{8}(x - 1)^2 + 2$$

Geometry iM KH

Lesson 8 Practice Problems

1. Classify the graph of the equation $x^2 + y^2 - 8x + 4y = 29$.

    A. circle

    B. exponential curve

    C. line

    D. parabola

2. Write an equation that states (x, y) is the same distance from $(4, 1)$ as it is from the x-axis.

3. Select **all** equations which describe the parabola with focus $(-1, -7)$ and directrix $y = 3$.

    A. $(x - 1)^2 + (y - 7)^2 = (y + 3)^2$

    B. $(x + 1)^2 + (y + 7)^2 = (y - 3)^2$

    C. $y = -20(x + 1)^2 - 2$

    D. $y = -20(x + 1)^2 + 2$

    E. $y = -\frac{1}{20}(x + 1)^2 - 2$

    F. $y = -\frac{1}{20}(x + 1)^2 + 2$

4. Parabola A and parabola B both have the x-axis as the directrix. Parabola A has its focus at $(3, 2)$ and parabola B has its focus at $(5, 4)$. Select **all** true statements.

   A. Parabola A is wider than parabola B.

   B. Parabola B is wider than parabola A.

   C. The parabolas have the same line of symmetry.

   D. The line of symmetry of parabola A is to the right of that of parabola B.

   E. The line of symmetry of parabola B is to the right of that of parabola A.

   (From Unit 6, Lesson 7.)

5. A parabola has focus $(5, 1)$ and directrix $y = -3$. Where is the parabola's vertex?

   (From Unit 6, Lesson 7.)

6. Select the value needed in the box in order for the expression to be a perfect square trinomial.

   $x^2 + 7x + \boxed{}$

   A. 3.5

   B. 7

   C. 12.25

   D. 14.5

   (From Unit 6, Lesson 6.)

7. Rewrite each expression as the product of 2 factors.

    a. $x^2 + 3x$

    b. $x^2 - 6x - 7$

    c. $x^2 + 4x + 4$

(From Unit 6, Lesson 5.)

8. Suppose this two-dimensional figure is rotated 360 degrees using the vertical axis shown. Each small square on the grid represents 1 square inch. What is the volume of the three-dimensional figure?

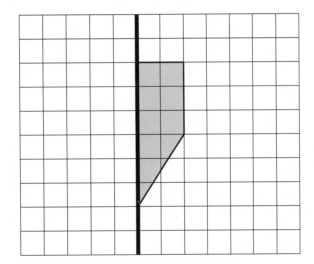

(From Unit 5, Lesson 15.)

Lesson 9: Equations of Lines

- Let's investigate equations of lines.

9.1: Remembering Slope

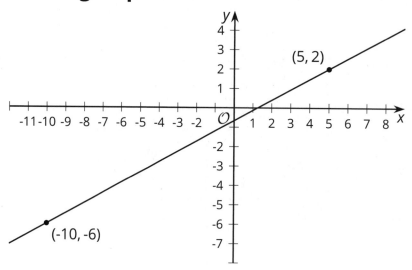

The slope of the line in the image is $\frac{8}{15}$. Explain how you know this is true.

9.2: Building an Equation for a Line

1. The image shows a line.

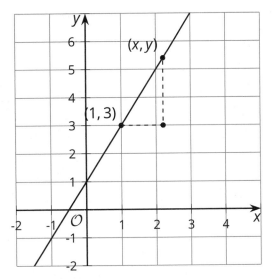

   a. Write an equation that says the slope between the points $(1, 3)$ and (x, y) is 2.

   b. Look at this equation: $y - 3 = 2(x - 1)$
      How does it relate to the equation you wrote?

2. Here is an equation for another line: $y - 7 = \frac{1}{2}(x - 5)$
   a. What point do you know this line passes through?

   b. What is the slope of this line?

3. Next, let's write a general equation that we can use for any line. Suppose we know a line passes through a particular point (h, k).
   a. Write an equation that says the slope between point (x, y) and (h, k) is m.

   b. Look at this equation: $y - k = m(x - h)$. How does it relate to the equation you wrote?

9.3: Using Point-Slope Form

1. Write an equation that describes each line.

   a. the line passing through point (-2, 8) with slope $\frac{4}{5}$

   b. the line passing through point (0, 7) with slope $-\frac{7}{3}$

   c. the line passing through point $(\frac{1}{2}, 0)$ with slope -1

   d. the line in the image

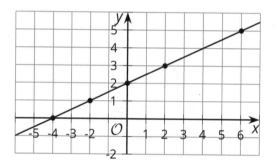

2. Using the structure of the equation, what point do you know each line passes through? What's the line's slope?

   a. $y - 5 = \frac{3}{2}(x + 4)$

   b. $y + 2 = 5x$

   c. $y = -2(x - \frac{5}{8})$

Are you ready for more?

Another way to describe a line, or other graphs, is to think about the coordinates as changing over time. This is especially helpful if we're thinking tracing an object's movement. This example describes the x- and y-coordinates separately, each in terms of time, t.

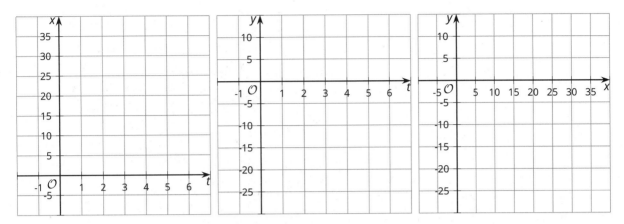

1. On the first grid, create a graph of $x = 2 + 5t$ for $-2 \leq t \leq 7$ with x on the vertical axis and t on the horizontal axis.

2. On the second grid, create a graph of $y = 3 - 4t$ for $-2 \leq t \leq 7$ with y on the vertical axis and t on the horizontal axis.

3. On the third grid, create a graph of the set of points $(2 + 5t, 3 - 4t)$ for $-2 \leq t \leq 7$ on the xy-plane.

Lesson 9 Summary

The line in the image can be defined as the set of points that have a slope of 2 with the point $(3, 4)$. An equation that says point (x, y) has slope 2 with $(3, 4)$ is $\frac{y-4}{x-3} = 2$. This equation can be rearranged to look like $y - 4 = 2(x - 3)$.

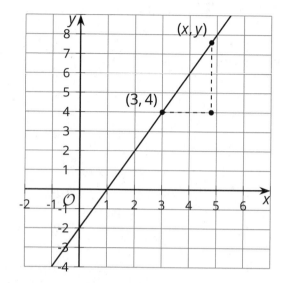

The equation is now in **point-slope form**, or $y - k = m(x - h)$, where:

- (x, y) is any point on the line

- (h, k) is a particular point on the line that we choose to substitute into the equation

- m is the slope of the line

Other ways to write the equation of a line include slope-intercept form, $y = mx + b$, and standard form, $Ax + By = C$.

To write the equation of a line passing through $(3, 1)$ and $(0, 5)$, start by finding the slope of the line. The slope is $-\frac{4}{3}$ because $\frac{5-1}{0-3} = -\frac{4}{3}$. Substitute this value for m to get $y - k = -\frac{4}{3}(x - h)$. Now we can choose any point on the line to substitute for (h, k). If we choose $(3, 1)$, we can write the equation of the line as $y - 1 = -\frac{4}{3}(x - 3)$.

We could also use $(0, 5)$ as the point, giving $y - 5 = -\frac{4}{3}(x - 0)$. We can rearrange the equation to see how point-slope and slope-intercept forms relate, getting $y = -\frac{4}{3}x + 5$. Notice $(0, 5)$ is the y-intercept of the line. The graphs of all 3 of these equations look the same.

Glossary

- point-slope form

Lesson 9 Practice Problems

1. Select **all** the equations that represent the graph shown.

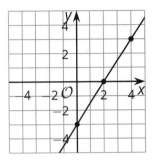

    A. $3x - 2y = 6$

    B. $y = \frac{3}{2}x + 3$

    C. $y = \frac{3}{2}x - 3$

    D. $y - 3 = \frac{3}{2}(x - 4)$

    E. $y - 6 = \frac{3}{2}(x - 2)$

2. A line with slope $\frac{3}{2}$ passes through the point $(1, 3)$.

    a. Explain why $(3, 6)$ is on this line.

    b. Explain why $(0, 0)$ is not on this line.

    c. Is the point $(13, 22)$ on this line? Explain why or why not.

3. Write an equation of the line that passes through $(1, 3)$ and has a slope of $\frac{5}{4}$.

4. A parabola has focus (3, -2) and directrix $y = 2$. The point $(a, -8)$ is on the parabola. How far is this point from the focus?

   A. 6 units

   B. 8 units

   C. 10 units

   D. cannot be determined

(From Unit 6, Lesson 8.)

5. Write an equation for a parabola with each given focus and directrix.

   a. focus: $(5, 2)$; directrix: x-axis

   b. focus: $(-2, 3)$; directrix: the line $y = 7$

   c. focus: $(0, 7)$; directrix: x-axis

   d. focus: $(-3, -4)$; directrix: the line $y = -1$

(From Unit 6, Lesson 8.)

6. A parabola has focus $(-1, 6)$ and directrix $y = 4$. Determine whether each point on the list is on this parabola. Explain your reasoning.

   a. $(-1, 5)$

   b. $(1, 7)$

   c. $(3, 9)$

(From Unit 6, Lesson 7.)

7. Select the center of the circle represented by the equation
$x^2 + y^2 - 8x + 11y - 2 = 0.$

   A. $(8, 11)$

   B. $(4, 5.5)$

   C. $(-4, -5.5)$

   D. $(4, -5.5)$

(From Unit 6, Lesson 6.)

8. Reflect triangle ABC over the line $x = $ -6.

   Translate the image by the directed line segment from $(0, 0)$ to $(5, $ -1$)$.

   What are the coordinates of the vertices in the final image?

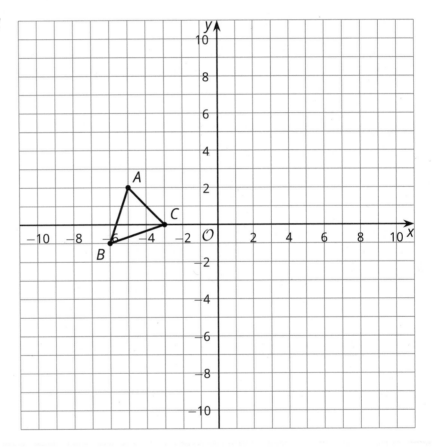

(From Unit 6, Lesson 1.)

Lesson 10: Parallel Lines in the Plane

- Let's investigate parallel lines in the coordinate plane.

10.1: Translating Lines

1. Draw any non-vertical line in the plane. Draw 2 possible translations of the line.

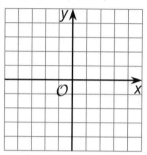

2. Find the slope of your original line and the slopes of the images.

10.2: Priya's Proof

Priya writes a proof saying:

Consider any 2 parallel lines. Assume they are not horizontal or vertical. Therefore they must pass through the x-axis as well as the y-axis. This forms 2 right triangles with a second congruent angle. Call the angle θ. The tangent of θ is equal for both triangles. Therefore the lines have the same slope.

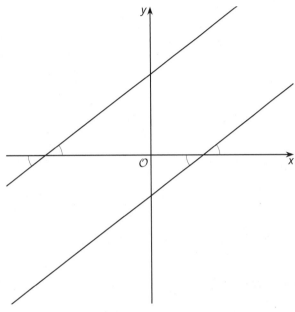

1. How does Priya know the right triangles have a second congruent angle?

2. Show or explain what it means that the tangent of θ is equal for both triangles.

3. How does this prove the slopes of parallel lines are equal?

10.3: Prove Your Parallelogram

1. Write the equation of a line parallel to $y = 2x + 3$, passing through (-4, 1).

2. Graph both lines described in the previous question.

3. Draw a parallelogram using the 2 lines you graphed and using (-4, 1) as one of the vertices.

4. Prove that your figure is a parallelogram.

Are you ready for more?

Prove algebraically that the translation $(x, y) \rightarrow (x + p, y + q)$ takes the line $y = mx + b$ to a line with the same slope.

Lesson 10 Summary

The solid line has been translated in 2 different ways:

1. by the directed line segment from $(2, 2)$ to $(2, 4)$ to produce the dashed line above

2. by the directed line segment from $(2, 2)$ to $(2, -2)$ to produce the dotted line below

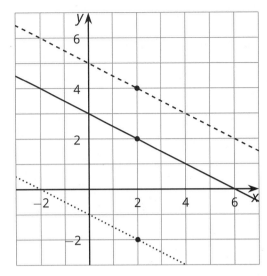

The 3 lines look parallel to one another, as we would expect. We know that translations of lines result in parallel lines.

What happens to the slopes of these lines? If we draw in the slope triangles that go through the origin, we can see right triangles. Since we know the lines are parallel, the corresponding pairs of angles in the triangles must be congruent by the Alternate Interior Angles Theorem. Triangles with congruent angles are similar, and similar slope triangles result in lines with the same slope. Here we see slopes of $-\frac{5}{10}$, $-\frac{3}{6}$, and $-\frac{1}{2}$, which are all equal.

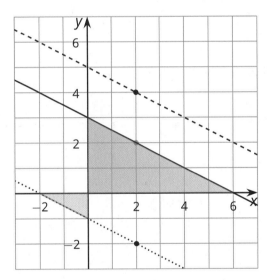

We can use similar reasoning to show that any 2 parallel lines that aren't vertical have the same slope, and also that any 2 lines with the same slope are parallel.

What if we wanted to find the equation of a line parallel to these 3 lines that goes through the point $(6, -1)$? We know the line must have the same slope of $-\frac{1}{2}$. We can use point-slope form and get $y + 1 = -\frac{1}{2}(x - 6)$.

Lesson 10 Practice Problems

1. Select **all** equations that are parallel to the line $2x + 5y = 8$.

   A. $y = \frac{2}{5}x + 4$

   B. $y = -\frac{2}{5}x + 4$

   C. $y - 2 = \frac{5}{2}(x + 1)$

   D. $y - 2 = -\frac{2}{5}(x + 1)$

   E. $10x + 5y = 40$

2. Prove that $ABCD$ is not a parallelogram.

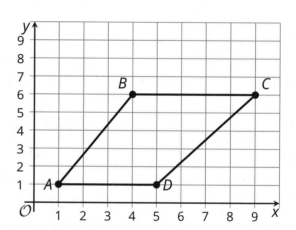

3. Write an equation of a line that passes through $(-1, 2)$ and is parallel to a line with x-intercept $(3, 0)$ and y-intercept $(0, 1)$.

4. Write an equation of the line with slope $\frac{2}{3}$ that goes through the point $(-2, 5)$.

   (From Unit 6, Lesson 9.)

5. Priya and Han each wrote an equation of a line with slope $\frac{1}{3}$ that passes through the point $(1, 2)$. Priya's equation is $y - 2 = \frac{1}{3}(x - 1)$ and Han's equation is $3y - x = 5$. Do you agree with either of them? Explain or show your reasoning.

(From Unit 6, Lesson 9.)

6. Match each equation with another equation whose graph is the same parabola.

A. $(x - 3)^2 + (y - 2)^2 = y^2$

B. $(x - 2)^2 + (y - 3)^2 = (y + 3)^2$

C. $(x - 3)^2 + (y - 4)^2 = (y + 2)^2$

D. $(x - 2)^2 + (y - 2)^2 = (y + 2)^2$

1. $y = \frac{1}{8}(x - 2)^2$

2. $y = \frac{1}{12}(x - 2)^2$

3. $y = \frac{1}{4}(x - 3)^2 + 1$

4. $y = \frac{1}{12}(x - 3)^2 + 1$

(From Unit 6, Lesson 8.)

7. A parabola is defined as the set of points the same distance from $(-1, 3)$ and the line $y = 5$. Select the point that is on this parabola.

   A. $(-1, 3)$

   B. $(0, 5)$

   C. $(3, 0)$

   D. $(0, 0)$

   (From Unit 6, Lesson 7.)

8. Here are some transformation rules. For each rule, describe whether the transformation is a rigid motion, a dilation, or neither.

   a. $(x, y) \rightarrow (2x, y + 2)$

   b. $(x, y) \rightarrow (2x, 2y)$

   c. $(x, y) \rightarrow (x + 2, y + 2)$

   d. $(x, y) \rightarrow (x - 2, y)$

   (From Unit 6, Lesson 2.)

Lesson 11: Perpendicular Lines in the Plane

- Let's analyze the slopes of perpendicular lines.

11.1: Revisiting Transformations

The image shows quadrilateral $ABCD$.

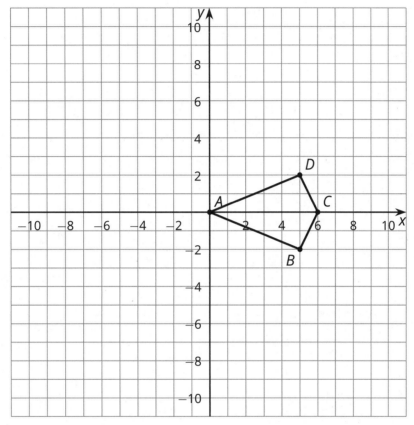

Apply the transformation rule $(x, y) \rightarrow (-y, x)$ to quadrilateral $ABCD$. What is the effect of the transformation rule?

11.2: Make a Conjecture

1. Complete the table with the slope of each segment from the warm-up.

	original figure slope	image slope	product
AB			
BC			
CD			
DA			

2. The image in the warm-up is a 90-degree rotation of the original figure, so each line in the original figure is perpendicular to the corresponding line in the image. Use your slope calculations to make a conjecture about slopes of perpendicular lines.

11.3: Prove It

Let's prove our conjecture about slopes of perpendicular lines for the case where the lines pass through the origin.

1. Find the slope of a line passing through the point (a, b) and the origin. Assume the line is not horizontal or vertical.

2. Suppose the line is rotated using the transformation rule $(x, y) \rightarrow (-y, x)$. Find the coordinates of the images of the points (a, b) and the origin.

3. How does the original line relate to the image?

4. Find the slope of the image.

5. Compare your slopes. What did you just prove?

Are you ready for more?

We can take any rhombus $EFGH$ and translate it so that the image of E is $(0,0)$. We can then rotate using $(0,0)$ as a center so that the image of F under this sequence is on the positive x-axis at some point $(c, 0)$.

1. Suppose these transformations take the point H to some point (a, b). What must the coordinates of G be?

2. For the values of a, b, and c in this problem, why is it true that $a^2 + b^2 = c^2$?

3. Prove that the diagonals of the image are perpendicular.

4. Prove that the diagonals of the image bisect each other.

5. Why does this imply the diagonals of **all** rhombi are perpendicular bisectors of each other?

Lesson 11 Summary

The diagram shows triangle ABC and its image, triangle $AB'C'$, under a 90-degree rotation counterclockwise using the origin as the center. Since the rotation was through 90 degrees, all line segments in the image are perpendicular to the corresponding segments in the original triangle. For example, segment AC is horizontal, while segment AC' is vertical.

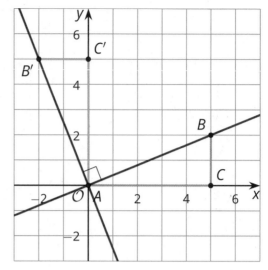

Look at segments AB and AB', which, like the other pairs of segments, are perpendicular. The slope of segment AB is $\frac{2}{5}$, while the slope of segment AB' is $-\frac{5}{2}$. Notice the relationship between the slopes: They are reciprocals of one another, and have opposite signs. The product of the slopes, $\frac{2}{5} \cdot \left(-\frac{5}{2}\right)$, is -1. As long as perpendicular lines are not horizontal or vertical, their slopes will be **opposite reciprocals** and have a product of -1.

We can use this fact to help write equations of lines. For example, try writing the equation of a line that passes through the point (23, -30) and is perpendicular to a line ℓ represented by $y = 3x + 5$. The slope of line ℓ is 3. The slope of any line perpendicular to line ℓ is the opposite reciprocal of 3, or $-\frac{1}{3}$. Substitute the point (23, -30) and the slope $-\frac{1}{3}$ into the point-slope form to get the equation $y - (-30) = -\frac{1}{3}(x - 23)$.

Glossary

- opposite
- reciprocal

Lesson 11 Practice Problems

1. Write an equation for a line that passes through the origin and is perpendicular to $y = 5x - 2$.

2. Match each line with a perpendicular line.

   A. $y = 5x + 2$

   B. $y - 2.25 = -2(x - 2)$

   C. the line through $(-1, 5)$ and $(1, 9)$

   1. the line through $(2, 12)$ and $(17, 9)$

   2. $y = -\frac{1}{2}x + 5$

   3. $2x - 4y = 10$

3. The rule $(x, y) \rightarrow (y, -x)$ takes a line to a perpendicular line. Select **all** the rules that take a line to a perpendicular line.

   A. $(x, y) \rightarrow (2y, -x)$

   B. $(x, y) \rightarrow (-y, -x)$

   C. $(x, y) \rightarrow (-y, x)$

   D. $(x, y) \rightarrow (0.5y, -2x)$

   E. $(x, y) \rightarrow (4y, -4x)$

4.   a. Write an equation of the line with x-intercept $(3, 0)$ and y-intercept $(0, -4)$.

   b. Write an equation of a line parallel to the line $y - 5 = \frac{4}{3}(x - 2)$.

   (From Unit 6, Lesson 10.)

5. Lines ℓ and p are parallel. Select **all** true statements.

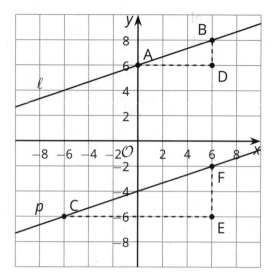

A. Triangle ADB is similar to triangle CEF.

B. Triangle ADB is congruent to triangle CEF.

C. The slope of line ℓ is equal to the slope of line p.

D. $\sin(A) = \sin(C)$

E. $\sin(B) = \cos(C)$

(From Unit 6, Lesson 10.)

6. Select the equation that states (x, y) is the same distance from $(0, 5)$ as it is from the line $y = -3$.

A. $x^2 + (y + 5)^2 = (y + 3)^2$

B. $x^2 + (y - 5)^2 = (y + 3)^2$

C. $x^2 + (y + 5)^2 = (y - 3)^2$

D. $x^2 + (y - 5)^2 = (y - 3)^2$

(From Unit 6, Lesson 8.)

7. Select **all** equations that represent the graph shown.

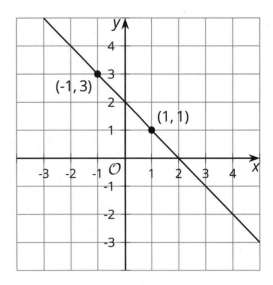

A. $y = -x + 2$

B. $(y - 3) = -(x + 1)$

C. $(y - 3) = -x - 1$

D. $(y - 3) = (x - 1)$

E. $(y + 1) = -(x - 3)$

(From Unit 6, Lesson 9.)

8. Write a rule that describes this transformation.

original figure	image
$(3, 2)$	$(6, 4)$
$(4, -1)$	$(8, -2)$
$(5, 1)$	$(10, 2)$
$(7, 3)$	$(14, 6)$

(From Unit 6, Lesson 3.)

Lesson 12: It's All on the Line

- Let's work with both parallel and perpendicular lines.

12.1: Parallel and Perpendicular

The image shows line n.

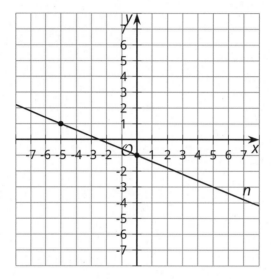

1. Write an equation for the line that is perpendicular to n and whose y-intercept is $(0, 5)$. Graph this line.

2. Write an equation for the line that is parallel to n and that passes through the point $(3, 1)$. Graph this line.

Geometry iM KH

12.2: Info Gap: Lines

Your teacher will give you either a problem card or a data card. Do not show or read your card to your partner.

If your teacher gives you the data card:

1. Silently read the information on your card.

2. Ask your partner, "What specific information do you need?" and wait for your partner to ask for information. Only give information that is on your card. (Do not figure out anything for your partner!)

3. Before telling your partner the information, ask, "Why do you need to know (that piece of information)?"

4. Read the problem card, and solve the problem independently.

5. Share the data card, and discuss your reasoning.

If your teacher gives you the problem card:

1. Silently read your card and think about what information you need to answer the question.

2. Ask your partner for the specific information that you need.

3. Explain to your partner how you are using the information to solve the problem.

4. When you have enough information, share the problem card with your partner, and solve the problem independently.

5. Read the data card, and discuss your reasoning.

Pause here so your teacher can review your work. Ask your teacher for a new set of cards and repeat the activity, trading roles with your partner.

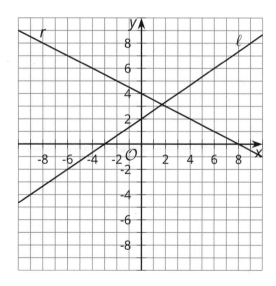

12.3: Three Lines

1. Line ℓ is represented by the equation $y = \frac{2}{3}x + 3$. Write an equation of the line perpendicular to ℓ, passing through $(-6, 4)$. Call this line p.

2. Write an equation of the line perpendicular to p, passing through $(3, -2)$. Call this line n.

3. What do you notice about lines ℓ and n? Does this always happen? Show or explain your answer.

Are you ready for more?

Prove that the line $Ax + By = C$ is always perpendicular to the line that passes through (A, B) and the origin.

Lesson 12 Summary

We can use the concepts of parallel and perpendicular lines to write equations of lines. The image shows line ℓ.

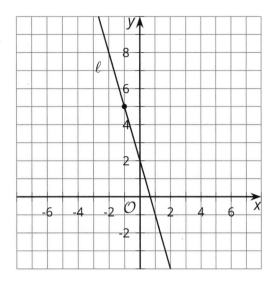

Suppose n is the image of ℓ when it is rotated 90 degrees using $(-1, 5)$ as a center. What is an equation of line n?

The point $(-1, 5)$ is on line ℓ. The center of rotation does not move when a figure is rotated, so $(-1, 5)$ will also be on the image, line n. Because line ℓ was rotated 90 degrees, lines ℓ and n are perpendicular. Their slopes must be opposite reciprocals. The slope of line ℓ is -3, so the slope of n is $\frac{1}{3}$. Now substitute the slope $\frac{1}{3}$ and the point $(-1, 5)$ into point-slope form to get $y - 5 = \frac{1}{3}(x - (-1))$.

Lesson 12 Practice Problems

1. For each equation, is the graph of the equation parallel to the line shown, perpendicular to the line shown, or neither?

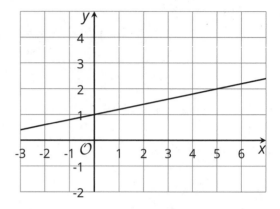

    a. $y = 0.2x$

    b. $y = -2x + 1$

    c. $y = 5x - 3$

    d. $(y - 3) = -5(x - 4)$

    e. $(y - 1) = 2(x - 3)$

    f. $5x + y = 3$

2. Main Street is parallel to Park Street. Park Street is parallel to Elm Street. Elm is perpendicular to Willow. How does Willow compare to Main?

3. The line which is the graph of $y = 2x - 4$ is transformed by the rule $(x, y) \rightarrow (-x, -y)$. What is the slope of the image?

4. Select **all** equations whose graphs are lines perpendicular to the graph of $3x + 2y = 6$.

    A. $3x - 2y = 4$

    B. $2x + 3y = 6$

    C. $2x - 3y = 8$

    D. $(y - 4) = \frac{2}{3}(x - 6)$

    E. $(y - 2) = -\frac{3}{2}(x - 8)$

    F. $y = \frac{2}{3}x$

    G. $y = \frac{3}{2}x + 3$

(From Unit 6, Lesson 11.)

5. Match each line with a perpendicular line.

    A. the line through $(12, 4)$ and $(9, 19)$ 1. the line through $(3, 1)$ and $(1, 4)$

    B. $2x - 5y = 10$ 2. $y = \frac{1}{5}x + 7$

    C. $y - 4 = \frac{2}{3}(x + 1)$ 3. $y - 1 = -2.5(x + 3)$

(From Unit 6, Lesson 11.)

6. The graph of $y = -4x + 2$ is translated by the directed line segment AB shown. What is the slope of the image?

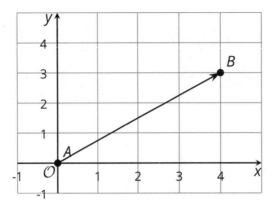

(From Unit 6, Lesson 10.)

7. Select **all** points on the line with a slope of $-\frac{1}{2}$ that go through the point $(4, -1)$.

   A. $(-2, 2)$

   B. $(0, 2)$

   C. $(4, -1)$

   D. $(0, 1)$

   E. $(-3, 8)$

(From Unit 6, Lesson 9.)

8. One way to define a circle is that it is the set of all points that are the same distance from a given center. How does the equation $(x - h)^2 + (y - k)^2 = r^2$ relate to this definition? Draw a diagram if it helps you explain.

(From Unit 6, Lesson 4.)

Lesson 13: Intersection Points

- Let's look at how circles and parabolas interact with lines.

13.1: Which One Doesn't Belong: Lines and Curves

Which one doesn't belong?

A

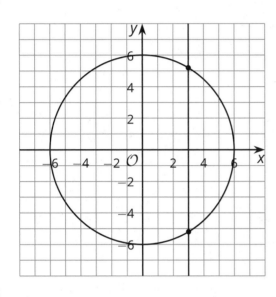

B

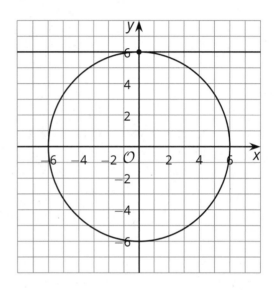

C

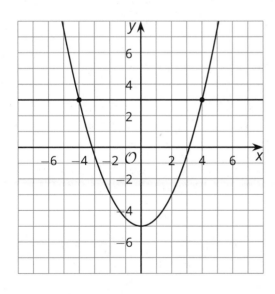

D

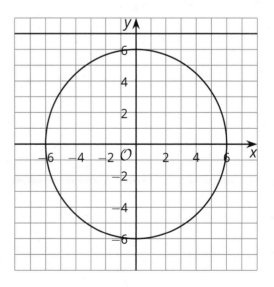

13.2: Circles and Lines

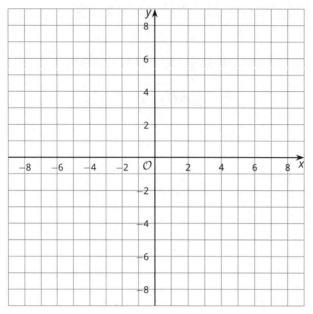

1. The equation $(x - 3)^2 + (y - 2)^2 = 25$ represents a circle. Graph this circle on the coordinate grid.

2. Graph the line $y = 6$. At what points does this line appear to intersect the circle?

3. How can you verify that the 2 figures really intersect at these points? Carry out whatever procedure you decide.

4. Graph the line $y = x - 2$. At what points does this line appear to intersect the circle? Verify that the 2 figures really do intersect at these points.

Geometry

13.3: Creating Lines

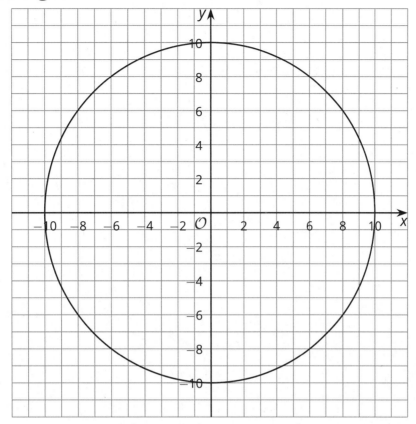

1. Write an equation representing the circle in the graph.

2. Graph and write equations for each line described:
   a. any line parallel to the *x*-axis that intersects the circle at 2 points

   b. any line perpendicular to the *x*-axis that doesn't intersect the circle

   c. the line perpendicular to $y = -\frac{1}{3}x + 5$ that intersects the circle at $(6, 8)$

3. For the last line you graphed, find the second point where the line intersects the circle. Explain or show your reasoning.

Are you ready for more?

1. Graph the equations $y - 3 = (x - 2)^2$ and $y - 4 = 2(x - 3)$ and find their point of intersection.

2. Show that the graph of $y - 3 = (x - 2)^2$ and $y - 4 = m(x - 3)$ intersect at the point $(m + 1, m^2 - 2m + 4)$.

Lesson 13 Summary

We can graph circles and lines on the same coordinate grid and estimate where they intersect. The image shows the circle $(x - 10)^2 + (y + 6)^2 = 169$ and the line $y = x - 23$. The 2 figures appear to intersect at the points (22, -1) and (5, -18). To verify whether these truly are intersection points, we can check if substituting them into each equation produces true statements.

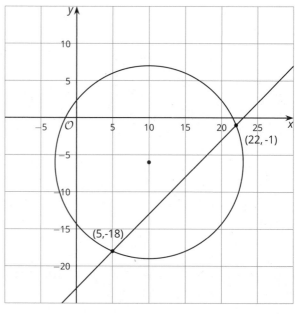

Let's test (22, -1). First, substitute it into the equation for the line. When we do so, we get -1 = 22 − 23. This is a true statement, so this point is on the line.

Next, substitute it into the equation for the circle. This is the same as checking to see if the distance from the point to the center is $\sqrt{169}$, or 13 units. We get $(22 - 10)^2 + (-1 - (-6))^2 = 169$. Evaluate the left side to get $144 + 25 = 169$. This is a true statement, so the point (22, -1) is on the circle. It's on both the circle and the line, so it must be an intersection point for the 2 figures.

Lesson 13 Practice Problems

1. Graph the equations $(x - 2)^2 + (y + 3)^2 = 36$ and $x = 2$. Where do they intersect?

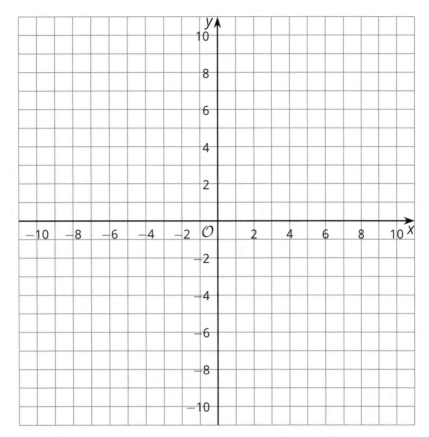

2. Select **all** equations for which the point (2, -3) is on the graph of the equation.

   A. $y - 3 = x - 2$

   B. $4x + y = 5$

   C. $y = 5x - 13$

   D. $x^2 + y^2 = 13$

   E. $(x - 2)^2 + (y - (-3))^2 = 25$

   F. $y = (x - 2)^2 + 3$

   G. $y = x^2 - 7$

3. The image shows a graph of the parabola with focus $(3, 4)$ and directrix $y = 2$, and the line given by $y = 4$. Find and verify the points where the parabola and the line intersect.

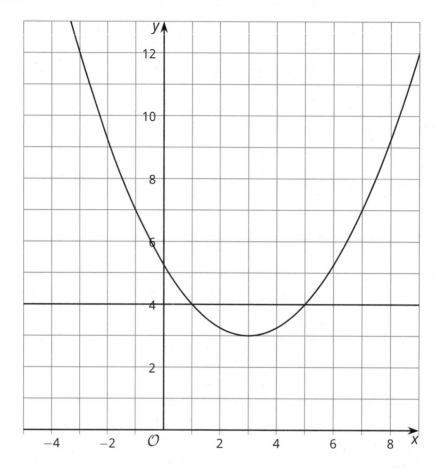

4. Here is a line ℓ. Write equations for and graph 4 different lines perpendicular to ℓ.

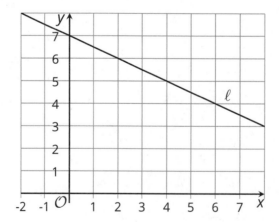

(From Unit 6, Lesson 12.)

Geometry iM **KH**

5. Write an equation whose graph is a line perpendicular to the graph of $y = 4$ and which passes through the point $(2, 5)$.

(From Unit 6, Lesson 12.)

6. Select **all** lines that are perpendicular to $y - 4 = -\frac{2}{3}(x + 1)$.

   A. $y = \frac{3}{2}x + 8$

   B. $3x - 2y = 2$

   C. $3x + 2y = 10$

   D. $y - 2 = -\frac{2}{3}(x - 1)$

   E. $y = \frac{3}{2}x$

(From Unit 6, Lesson 11.)

7. Select the line parallel to $3x - 2y = 10$.

   A. $y - 1 = \frac{3}{2}(x + 6)$

   B. $6x + 4y = -20$

   C. $y = -\frac{3}{2}x + 2$

   D. $y - 4 = \frac{2}{3}(x + 1)$

(From Unit 6, Lesson 10.)

8. Explain how you could tell whether $x^2 + bx + c$ is a perfect square trinomial.

(From Unit 6, Lesson 5.)

Lesson 14: Coordinate Proof

- Let's use coordinates to prove theorems and to compute perimeter and area.

14.1: Which One Doesn't Belong: Coordinate Quadrilaterals

Which one doesn't belong?

A

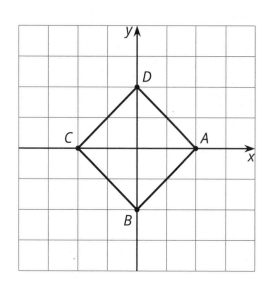

B

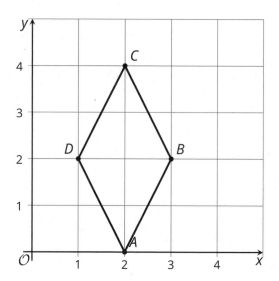

C

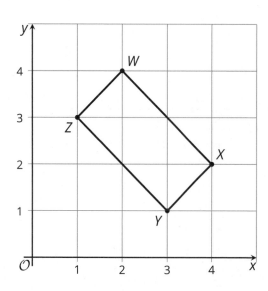

D

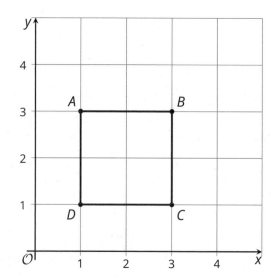

Geometry **iM KH**

14.2: Name This Quadrilateral

A quadrilateral has vertices $(0, 0), (4, 3), (13, -9)$, and $(9, -12)$.

1. What type of quadrilateral is it? Explain or show your reasoning.

2. Find the perimeter of this quadrilateral.

3. Find the area of this quadrilateral.

Are you ready for more?

1. A parallelogram has vertices $(0, 0), (5, 1), (2, 3)$, and $(7, 4)$. Find the area of this parallelogram.

2. Consider a general parallelogram with vertices $(0, 0), (a, b), (c, d)$, and $(a + c, b + d)$, where a, b, c, and d are positive. Write an expression for its area in terms of a, b, c, and d.

14.3: Circular Logic

The image shows a circle with several points plotted on the circle.

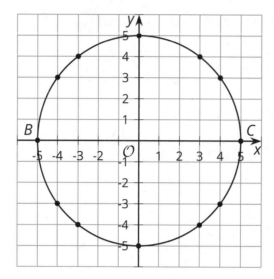

1. What kind of segment is BC in reference to the circle?

2. Choose one of the plotted points on the circle and call it D. Each student in the group should choose a different point. Draw segments BD and DC. What does the measure of angle BDC appear to be?

3. Calculate the slopes of segments BD and DC. What do your results tell you?

4. Compare your results to those of others in your group. What did they find?

5. Based on your group's results, write a conjecture that captures what you are seeing.

Geometry iM KH

Lesson 14 Summary

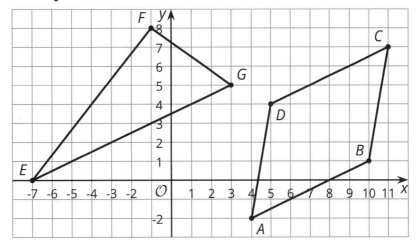

What kind of shape is quadrilateral $ABCD$? It looks like it might be a rhombus. To check, we can calculate the length of each side. Using the Pythagorean Theorem, we find that the lengths of segments AB and CD are $\sqrt{45}$ units, and the lengths of segments BC and DA are $\sqrt{37}$ units. All side lengths are between 6 and 7 units long, but they are not exactly the same. So our calculations show that $ABCD$ is not really a rhombus, even though at first glance we might think it is.

We did just show that two pairs of opposite sides of $ABCD$ are congruent. This means that $ABCD$ must be a parallelogram. Checking slopes confirms this. Sides AB and CD each have slope $\frac{1}{2}$. Sides BC and DA each have slope 6.

Can we find the area of triangle EFG? That seems tricky, because we don't know the height of the triangle using EG as the base. However, angle EFG seems like it could be a right angle. In that case, we could use sides EF and FG as the base and height.

To see if EFG is a right angle, we can calculate slopes. The slope of EF is $\frac{8}{6}$ or $\frac{4}{3}$, and the slope of FG is $-\frac{3}{4}$. Since the slopes are opposite reciprocals, the segments are perpendicular and angle EFG is indeed a right angle. This means that we can think of EF as the base and FG as the height. The length of EF is 10 units and the length of FG is 5 units. So the area of triangle EFG is 25 square units because $\frac{1}{2} \cdot 10 \cdot 5 = 25$.

Lesson 14 Practice Problems

1. A quadrilateral has vertices $A = (0, 0)$, $B = (1, 3)$, $C = (0, 4)$, and $D = (-1, 1)$. Prove that $ABCD$ is a parallelogram.

2. A rhombus has vertices at $(0, 0)$, $(5, 0)$, $(3, 4)$, and $(8, 4)$.

    a. Find the slopes of the 2 diagonals of the rhombus.

    b. What do the slopes tell you about the diagonals in this rhombus?

3.   a. Show that the triangle formed with vertices at $(0, 0)$, $(4, 3)$, and $(-2, 11)$ is a right triangle.

    b. Find the area of the triangle.

Geometry

4. For each pair of figures, at how many points is it possible that they intersect? List all possibilities.

   a. two distinct lines

   b. a line and a circle

   c. a line and a parabola

(From Unit 6, Lesson 13.)

5. Here are the graphs of the circle centered at $(0, 0)$ with radius 8 and the line given by $4x + 7y = 65$. Determine whether the circle and the line intersect at the point $(4, 7)$.

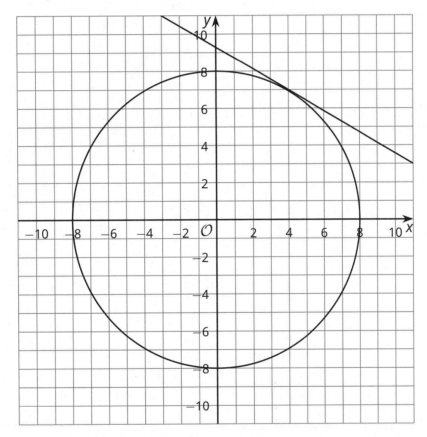

(From Unit 6, Lesson 13.)

6. Here is a line ℓ. Write equations for and graph 2 different lines perpendicular to ℓ and 2 different lines parallel to ℓ.

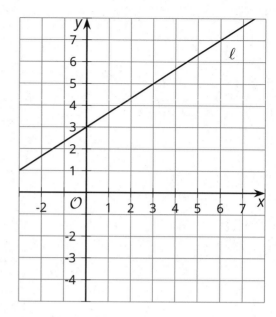

(From Unit 6, Lesson 12.)

7. The line shown is rotated 90 degrees clockwise around the origin. What is the slope of its image?

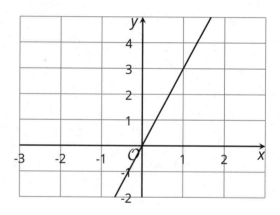

(From Unit 6, Lesson 11.)

Geometry

8. Elena is writing an explanation on completing the square for circle equations for Diego because he missed class. Here is what Elena wrote:

"Suppose we want to rewrite an equation in the form $(x - h)^2 + (y - k)^2 = r^2$. First, move any numbers to the right side and group terms with the same variables together on the left. Second, figure out what must be added to the set of x-terms and the set of y-terms to create 2 perfect square trinomials. Add those numbers to both the left and right sides of the equation. Next, rewrite the perfect square trinomials as squared binomials, and rewrite the right side in the form r^2. The center and radius can now be read directly from the equation."

Diego is unsure how to determine what needs to be added in order to get 2 perfect square trinomials. Explain how to determine the values.

(From Unit 6, Lesson 6.)

9. The semaphore alphabet is a way to use flags to signal messages. Here's how to signal the letter U. Describe a transformation that would take the left hand flag to the right hand flag.

U

(From Unit 1, Lesson 13.)

Lesson 15: Weighted Averages

- Let's split segments using averages and ratios.

15.1: Part Way: Points

For the questions in this activity, use the coordinate grid if it is helpful to you.

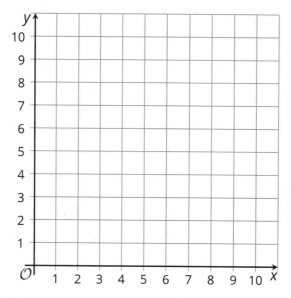

1. What is the midpoint of the segment connecting $(1, 2)$ and $(5, 2)$?

2. What is the midpoint of the segment connecting $(5, 2)$ and $(5, 10)$?

3. What is the midpoint of the segment connecting $(1, 2)$ and $(5, 10)$?

Geometry iM KH

15.2: Part Way: Segment

Point A has coordinates $(2, 4)$. Point B has coordinates $(8, 1)$.

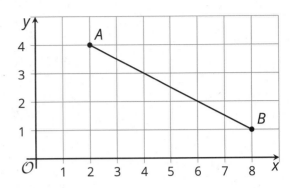

1. Find the point that partitions segment AB in a $2 : 1$ ratio.

2. Calculate $C = \frac{1}{3}A + \frac{2}{3}B$.

3. What do you notice about your answers to the first 2 questions?

4. For 2 new points K and L, write an expression for the point that partitions segment KL in a $3 : 1$ ratio.

Are you ready for more?

Consider the general quadrilateral $QRST$ with $Q = (0, 0)$, $R = (a, b)$, $S = (c, d)$, and $T = (e, f)$.

1. Find the midpoints of each side of this quadrilateral.

2. Show that if these midpoints are connected consecutively, the new quadrilateral formed is a parallelogram.

15.3: Part Way: Quadrilateral

Here is quadrilateral $ABCD$.

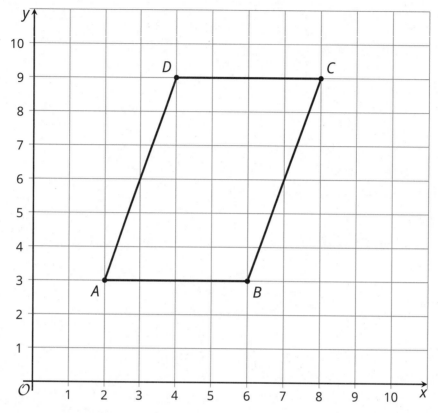

1. Find the point that partitions segment AB in a 1 : 4 ratio. Label it B'.

2. Find the point that partitions segment AD in a 1 : 4 ratio. Label it D'.

3. Find the point that partitions segment AC in a 1 : 4 ratio. Label it C'.

4. Is $AB'C'D'$ a dilation of $ABCD$? Justify your answer.

Lesson 15 Summary

To find the midpoint of a line segment, we can average the coordinates of the endpoints. For example, to find the midpoint of the segment from $A = (0, 4)$ to $B = (6, 7)$, average the coordinates of A and B: $\left(\frac{0+6}{2}, \frac{4+7}{2}\right) = (3, 5.5)$. Another way to write what we just did is $\frac{1}{2}(A + B)$ or $\frac{1}{2}A + \frac{1}{2}B$.

Now, let's find the point that is $\frac{2}{3}$ of the way from A to B. In other words, we'll find point C so that segments AC and CB are in a $2 : 1$ ratio.

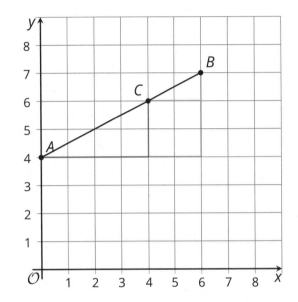

In the horizontal direction, segment AB stretches from $x = 0$ to $x = 6$. The distance from 0 to 6 is 6 units, so we calculate $\frac{2}{3}$ of 6 to get 4. Point C will be 4 horizontal units away from A, which means an x-coordinate of 4.

In the vertical direction, segment AB stretches from $y = 4$ to $y = 7$. The distance from 4 to 7 is 3 units, so we can calculate $\frac{2}{3}$ of 3 to get 2. Point C must be 2 vertical units away from A, which means a y-coordinate of 6.

It is possible to do this all at once by saying $C = \frac{1}{3}A + \frac{2}{3}B$. This is called a weighted average. Instead of finding the point in the middle, we want to find a point closer to B than to A. So we give point B more weight—it has a coefficient of $\frac{2}{3}$ rather than $\frac{1}{2}$ as in the midpoint calculation. To calculate $C = \frac{1}{3}A + \frac{2}{3}B$, substitute and evaluate.

$\frac{1}{3}A + \frac{2}{3}B$

$\frac{1}{3}(0, 4) + \frac{2}{3}(6, 7)$

$\left(0, \frac{4}{3}\right) + \left(4, \frac{14}{3}\right)$

$(4, 6)$

Either way, we found that the coordinates of C are $(4, 6)$.

Lesson 15 Practice Problems

1. Consider the parallelogram with vertices at $(0,0), (4,0), (2,3)$, and $(6,3)$. Where do the diagonals of this parallelogram intersect?

   A. $(3, 1.5)$

   B. $(4, 2)$

   C. $(2, 4)$

   D. $(3.5, 3)$

2. What is the midpoint of the line segment with endpoints $(1, -2)$ and $(9, 8)$?

   A. $(3, 5)$

   B. $(4, 3)$

   C. $(5, 3)$

   D. $(5, 5)$

3. Graph the image of triangle ABC under a dilation with center A and scale factor $\frac{2}{3}$.

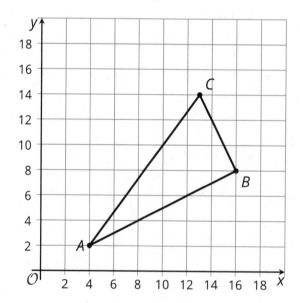

Geometry iM **KH**

4. A quadrilateral has vertices $A = (0,0)$, $B = (2,4)$, $C = (0,5)$, and $D = (-2,1)$. Prove that $ABCD$ is a rectangle.

(From Unit 6, Lesson 14.)

5. A quadrilateral has vertices $A = (0,0)$, $B = (1,3)$, $C = (0,4)$, and $D = (-1,1)$. Select the most precise classification for quadrilateral $ABCD$.

   A. quadrilateral

   B. parallelogram

   C. rectangle

   D. square

(From Unit 6, Lesson 14.)

6. Write an equation whose graph is a line perpendicular to the graph of $x = -7$ and which passes through the point $(-7, 1)$.

(From Unit 6, Lesson 12.)

7. Graph the equations $(x + 1)^2 + (y - 1)^2 = 64$ and $y = 1$. Where do they intersect?

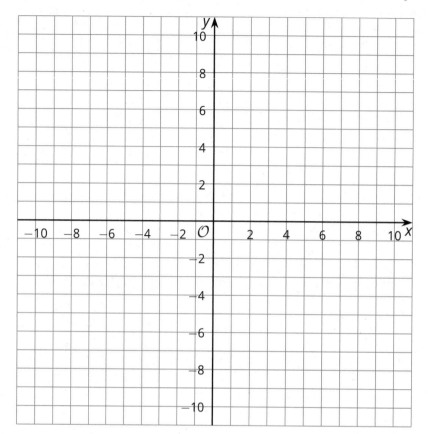

(From Unit 6, Lesson 13.)

8. A parabola has a focus of $(2, 5)$ and a directrix of $y = 1$. Decide whether each point on the list is on this parabola. Explain your reasoning.

a. $(-1, 5)$

b. $(2, 3)$

c. $(6, 6)$

(From Unit 6, Lesson 7.)

Geometry iM KH

Lesson 16: Weighted Averages in a Triangle

- Let's partition special line segments in triangles.

16.1: Triangle Midpoints

Triangle ABC is graphed.

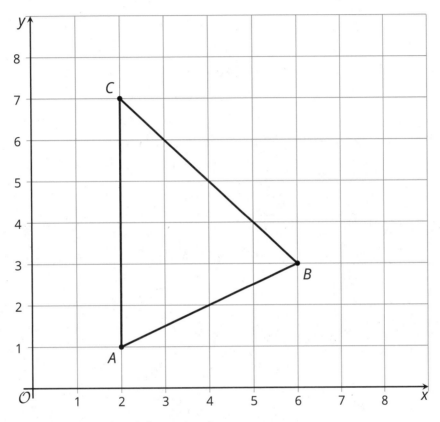

Find the midpoint of each side of this triangle.

16.2: Triangle Medians

Your teacher will tell you how to draw and label the **medians** of the triangle in the warm-up.

1. After the medians are drawn and labeled, measure all 6 segments inside the triangle using centimeters. What is the ratio of the 2 parts of each median?

2. Find the coordinates of the point that partitions segment AN in a $2 : 1$ ratio.

3. Find the coordinates of the point that partitions segment BL in a $2 : 1$ ratio.

4. Find the coordinates of the point that partitions segment CM in a $2 : 1$ ratio.

Are you ready for more?

In the image, AB is a median.

Find the length of AB in terms of a, b, and c.

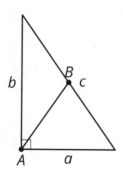

16.3: Any Triangle's Medians

The goal is to prove that the medians of any triangle intersect at a point. Suppose the vertices of a triangle are $(0, 0), (w, 0)$, and (a, b).

1. Each student in the group should choose 1 side of the triangle. If your group has 4 people, 2 can work together. Write an expression for the midpoint of the side you chose.

2. Each student in the group should choose a median. Write an expression for the point that partitions each median in a $2 : 1$ ratio from the vertex to the midpoint of the opposite side.

3. Compare the coordinates of the point you found to those of your groupmates. What do you notice?

4. Explain how these steps prove that the 3 medians of any triangle intersect at a single point.

Lesson 16 Summary

Here is a triangle with its **medians** drawn in. A median is a line segment drawn from a vertex of a triangle to the midpoint of the opposite side. Triangles have 3 medians, with 1 for each vertex.

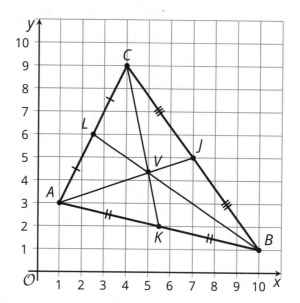

Notice that the medians intersect at 1 point. This point is always $\frac{2}{3}$ of the distance from a vertex to the opposite midpoint. Another way to say this is that the point of intersection, V, partitions segments AJ, BL, and CK so that the ratios $AV : VJ$, $BV : VL$, and $CV : VK$ are all $2 : 1$.

We can prove this by working with a general triangle that can represent any triangle. Since any triangle can be transformed so that 1 vertex is on the origin and 1 side lies on the x-axis, we can say that our general triangle has vertices $(0, 0)$, $(0, w)$, and (a, b). Through careful calculation, we can show that all 3 medians go through the point $\left(\frac{a+w}{3}, \frac{b}{3} \right)$. Therefore, the medians intersect at this point, which partitions each median in a $2 : 1$ ratio from the vertex to the opposite side's midpoint.

Glossary

- median (geometry)

Lesson 16 Practice Problems

1. Triangle ABC and its medians are shown.

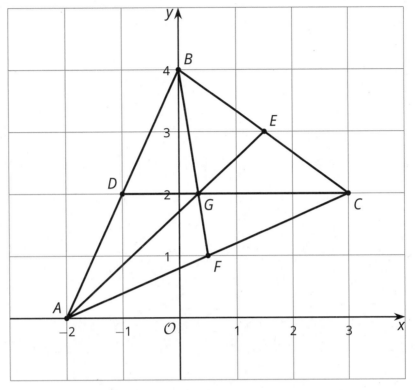

Select **all** statements that are true.

A. The medians intersect at $\left(\frac{1}{3}, 2\right)$.

B. The medians and altitudes are the same for this triangle.

C. An equation for median AE is $y = \frac{6}{7}(x + 2)$.

D. Point G is $\frac{2}{3}$ of the way from A to E.

E. Median BF is congruent to median CD.

2. Triangle ABC has vertices at $(-2, 0)$, $(-1, 6)$, and $(6, 0)$. What is the point of intersection of the triangle's medians?

3. Triangle EFG and its medians are shown.

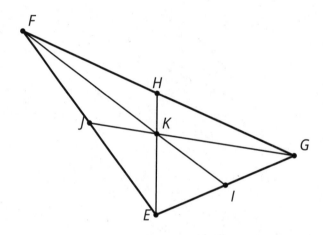

Match each pair of segments with the ratios of their lengths.

A. $GK : KJ$ 1. $1 : 1$

B. $GH : HF$ 2. $1 : 2$

C. $HK : KE$ 3. $2 : 1$

4. Given $A = (-3, 2)$ and $B = (7, -10)$, find the point that partitions segment AB in a $1 : 4$ ratio.

(From Unit 6, Lesson 15.)

Geometry iM KH

5. Graph the image of quadrilateral $ABCD$ under a dilation using center A and scale factor $\frac{1}{3}$.

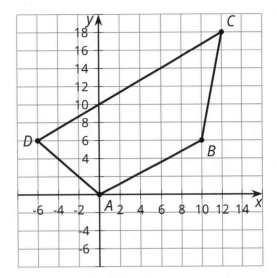

(From Unit 6, Lesson 15.)

6. A trapezoid is a quadrilateral with at least one pair of parallel sides. Show that the quadrilateral formed by the vertices $(0, 0)$, $(5, 2)$, $(10, 10)$, and $(0, 6)$ is a trapezoid.

(From Unit 6, Lesson 14.)

7. Here are the graphs of the circle centered at $(0, 0)$ with radius 6 units and the line given by $2x + y = 11$. Determine whether the circle and the line intersect at the point $(3, 5)$. Explain or show your reasoning.

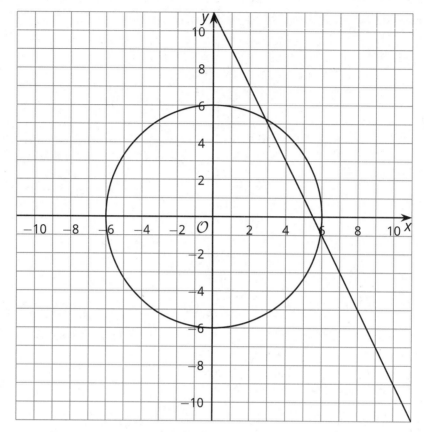

(From Unit 6, Lesson 13.)

8. A parabola has focus $(-3, 2)$ and directrix $y = -3$. The point $(a, 5)$ is on the parabola. How far is this point from the focus?

A. 8 units

B. 5 units

C. 3 units

D. 2 units

(From Unit 6, Lesson 8.)

Geometry iM KH

Lesson 17: Lines in Triangles

- Let's investigate more special segments in triangles.

17.1: Folding Altitudes

Draw a triangle on tracing paper. Fold the altitude from each vertex.

17.2: Altitude Attributes

Triangle ABC is graphed.

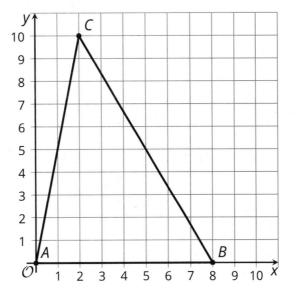

1. Find the slope of each side of the triangle.

2. Find the slope of each altitude of the triangle.

3. Sketch the altitudes. Label the point of intersection H.

4. Write equations for all 3 altitudes.

5. Use the equations to find the coordinates of H and verify algebraically that the altitudes all intersect at H.

Are you ready for more?

Any triangle ABC can be translated, rotated, and dilated so that the image A' lies on the origin, B' lies on the point $(1, 0)$, and C' has position (a, b). Use this as a starting point to prove that the altitudes of all triangles all meet at the same point.

17.3: Percolating on Perpendicular Bisectors

Triangle ABC is graphed.

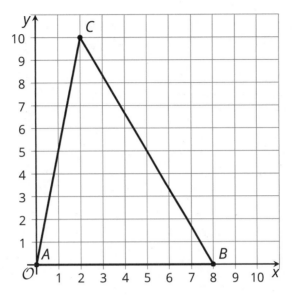

1. Find the midpoint of each side of the triangle.

2. Sketch the perpendicular bisectors, using an index card to help draw 90 degree angles. Label the intersection point P.

3. Write equations for all 3 perpendicular bisectors.

4. Use the equations to find the coordinates of P and verify algebraically that the perpendicular bisectors all intersect at P.

17.4: Perks of Perpendicular Bisectors

Consider triangle ABC from an earlier activity.

1. What is the distance from A to P, the intersection point of the perpendicular bisectors of the triangle's sides? Round to the nearest tenth.

2. Write the equation of a circle with center P and radius AP.

3. Construct the circle. What do you notice?

4. Verify your hypothesis algebraically.

17.5: Amazing Points

Consider triangle ABC from earlier activities.

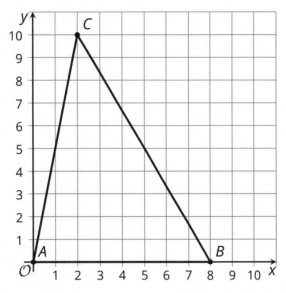

1. Plot point H, the intersection point of the altitudes.

2. Plot point P, the intersection point of the perpendicular bisectors.

3. Find the point where the 3 medians of the triangle intersect. Plot this point and label it J.

4. What seems to be true about points H, P, and J? Prove that your observation is true.

17.6: Tiling the (Coordinate) Plane

A tessellation covers the entire plane with shapes that do not overlap or leave gaps.

1. Tile the plane with congruent rectangles:
    a. Draw the rectangles on your grid.

    b. Write the equations for lines that outline 1 rectangle.

2. Tile the plane with congruent right triangles:
    a. Draw the right triangles on your grid.

    b. Write the equations for lines that outline 1 right triangle.

3. Tile the plane with any other shapes:
    a. Draw the shapes on your grid.

    b. Write the equations for lines that outline 1 of the shapes.

Lesson 17 Summary

The 3 medians of a triangle always intersect in 1 point. We can use coordinate geometry to show that the altitudes of a triangle intersect in 1 point, too. The 3 altitudes of triangle ABC are shown here. They appear to intersect at the point $(4, 6)$. By finding their equations, we can prove this is true.

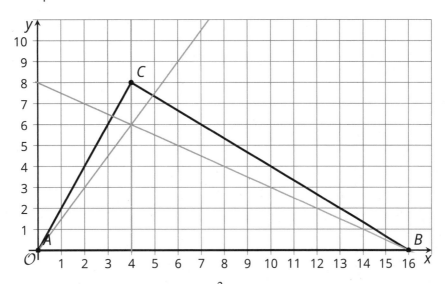

The slopes of sides AB, BC, and AC are 0, $-\frac{2}{3}$, and 2. The altitude from C is the vertical line $x = 4$. The slope of the altitude from A is $\frac{3}{2}$. Since the altitude goes through $(0, 0)$, its equation is $y = \frac{3}{2}x$. The slope of the altitude from B is $-\frac{1}{2}$. Following this slope over to the y-axis we can see that the y-intercept is 8. So the equation for this altitude is $y = -\frac{1}{2}x + 8$.

We can now verify that $(4, 6)$ lies on all 3 altitudes by showing that the point satisfies the 3 equations. By substitution we see that each equation is true when $x = 4$ and $y = 6$.

Lesson 17 Practice Problems

1. The 3 lines $x = 3$, $y - 2.5 = -\frac{1}{5}(x - 0.5)$, and $y - 2.5 = x - 3.5$ intersect at point P. Find the coordinates of P. Verify algebraically that the lines all intersect at P.

2. Triangle ABC has vertices at $(0, 0)$, $(5, 5)$, and $(10, 1)$. Kiran calculates the point of intersection of the medians using the following steps:

    a. Draw the triangle.

    b. Calculate the midpoint of each side.

    c. Draw the medians.

    d. Write an equation for 2 of the medians.

    e. Solve the system of equations.

    Use Kiran's method to calculate the point of intersection of the medians.

(From Unit 6, Lesson 16.)

Geometry iᴍ KH

3. Triangle ABC and its medians are shown. Write an equation for median AE.

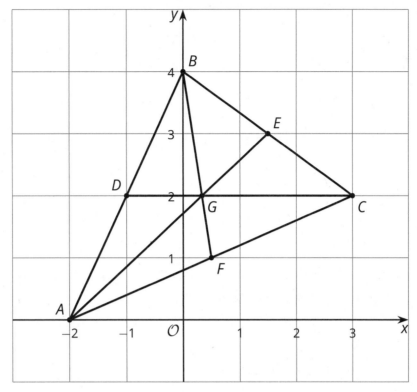

(From Unit 6, Lesson 16.)

4. Given $A = (1, 2)$ and $B = (7, 14)$, find the point that partitions segment AB in a $2 : 1$ ratio.

(From Unit 6, Lesson 15.)

5. A quadrilateral has vertices $A = (0, 0)$, $B = (4, 6)$, $C = (0, 12)$, and $D = (-4, 6)$. Mai thinks the quadrilateral is a rhombus and Elena thinks the quadrilateral is a square. Do you agree with either of them? Show or explain your reasoning.

(From Unit 6, Lesson 14.)

6. The image shows a graph of the parabola with focus (-3, -2) and directrix $y = 2$, and the line given by $y = -3$. Find and verify the points where the parabola and the line intersect.

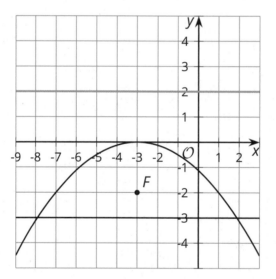

(From Unit 6, Lesson 13.)

Geometry iM KH

7. For each equation, is the graph of the equation parallel to the line shown, perpendicular to the line shown, or neither?

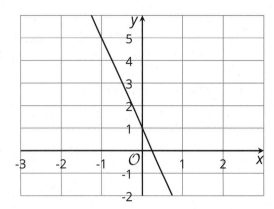

a. $y = 0.25x$

b. $y = 2x - 4$

c. $y - 2 = -4(x - 3)$

d. $2y + 8x = 7$

e. $x - 4y = 3$

(From Unit 6, Lesson 12.)

8. Write 2 equivalent equations for a line with x-intercept $(3, 0)$ and y-intercept $(0, 2)$.

(From Unit 6, Lesson 9.)

9. Parabola A and parabola B both have the line $y = -2$ as the directrix. Parabola A has its focus at $(3, 4)$ and parabola B has its focus at $(5, 0)$. Select **all** true statements.

A. Parabola A is wider than parabola B.

B. Parabola B is wider than parabola A.

C. The parabolas have the same line of symmetry.

D. The line of symmetry of parabola A is to the right of that of parabola B.

E. The line of symmetry of parabola B is to the right of that of parabola A.

(From Unit 6, Lesson 7.)

Learning Targets

Lesson 1: Rigid Transformations in the Plane

- I can prove triangles are congruent using coordinates.

- I can reflect, rotate, and translate figures in the coordinate plane.

Lesson 2: Transformations as Functions

- I can use coordinate transformation notation to take points in the plane as inputs and give other points as outputs.

Lesson 3: Types of Transformations

- I can determine whether a transformation produces congruent or similar images (or neither).

Lesson 4: Distances and Circles

- I can derive an equation for a circle in the coordinate plane.

Lesson 5: Squares and Circles

- I understand how squared binomials relate to the equation of a circle.

Lesson 6: Completing the Square

- I can complete the square to find the center and radius of a circle.

Lesson 7: Distances and Parabolas

- I know that a parabola is the set of points equidistant from a given point and line.

Lesson 8: Equations and Graphs

- I can derive an equation for a parabola in the coordinate plane given a focus and a directrix.

Lesson 9: Equations of Lines

- I can use the definition of slope to write the equation for a line in point-slope form.

Lesson 10: Parallel Lines in the Plane

- I can prove that the slopes of parallel lines are equal.

- I can use slopes of parallel lines to solve problems.

Lesson 11: Perpendicular Lines in the Plane

- I can prove that the slopes of perpendicular lines are opposite reciprocals.

- I can use slopes of perpendicular lines to solve problems.

Lesson 12: It's All on the Line

- I can gather information about a line and write its equation.

Lesson 13: Intersection Points

- I can use a graph to find the intersection points of a line and a circle.

Lesson 14: Coordinate Proof

- I can use coordinates of figures to prove geometric theorems.

Lesson 15: Weighted Averages

- I can calculate the coordinates of a point on a line segment that partitions the segment in a given ratio.

Lesson 16: Weighted Averages in a Triangle

- I can determine the point where the medians of a triangle intersect.

Lesson 17: Lines in Triangles

- I can determine the point where the altitudes of a triangle intersect.

Kendall Hunt

Illustrative Mathematics

GEOMETRY

Unit 7

STUDENT WORKBOOK
Book 3

Lesson 1: Lines, Angles, and Curves

- Let's define some line segments and angles related to circles.

1.1: Notice and Wonder: Lines and Angles

What do you notice? What do you wonder?

Geometry iM KH

1.2: The Defining Moment

1. The images show some line segments that are **chords** and some segments that are not chords.

   chords

   not chords

   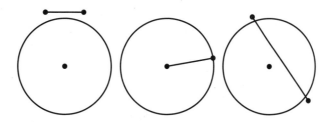

   Write a definition of a chord.

2. The images show some highlighted objects that are **arcs**, and some highlighted objects that are not arcs.

arcs

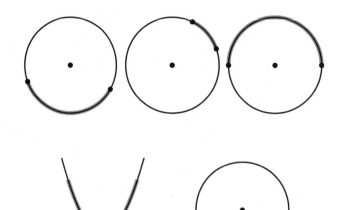

not arcs

Write a definition of an arc.

3. The images show some angles that are **central angles**, and some that are not.

central angles

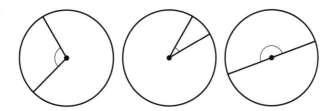

not central angles

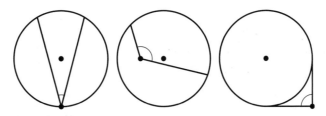

Write a definition of a central angle.

1.3: Arcs, Chords, and Central Angles

The image shows a circle with 2 congruent chords.

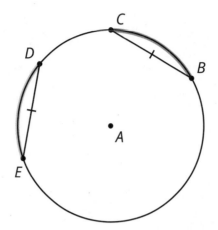

1. Draw the central angles associated with the highlighted arcs from D to E and B to C.

2. How do the measures of the 2 central angles appear to compare? Prove that this observation is true.

3. What does this tell you about the measures of the highlighted arcs from D to E and B to C? Explain your reasoning.

Are you ready for more?

Prove that the perpendicular bisector of a chord goes through the center of a circle.

Lesson 1 Summary

Diameters and radii are 2 types of line segments that appear in circles. Here are some additional geometric objects associated with circles.

A **chord** is a line segment whose endpoints are on the circle. A **central angle** in a circle is an angle whose vertex is at the center of the circle. An **arc** is the portion of a circle between 2 points on the circle. The measure of an arc is defined as the measure of the central angle formed by the radii drawn to the endpoints of the arc. For example, in the image, the highlighted arc between points D and E measures 45 degrees because the central angle DAE measures 45 degrees.

chord GH central angle PQR arc DE

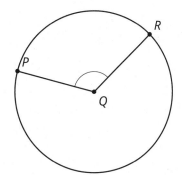
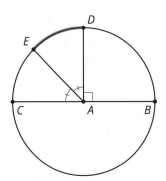

Glossary

- arc
- central angle
- chord

Lesson 1 Practice Problems

1. Find the values of x, y, and z.

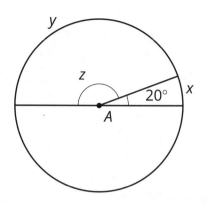

2. Give an example from the image of each kind of segment.

   a. a diameter

   b. a chord that is not a diameter

   c. a radius

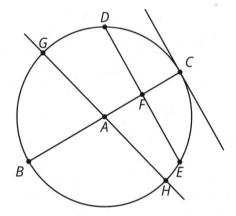

3. Identify whether each statement must be true, could possibly be true, or definitely can't be true.

   a. A diameter is a chord.

   b. A radius is a chord.

   c. A chord is a diameter.

   d. A central angle measures 90°.

Geometry i📐 **KH**

4. Write an equation of the altitude from vertex A.

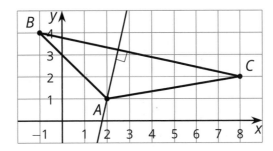

(From Unit 6, Lesson 17.)

5. Triangle ABC has vertices at $(5, 0), (1, 6)$, and $(9, 3)$. What is the point of intersection of the triangle's medians?

   A. The medians do not intersect in a single point.

   B. $(3, 3)$

   C. $(5, 3)$

   D. $(3, 4.5)$

(From Unit 6, Lesson 16.)

6. Consider the parallelogram with vertices at $(0, 0), (8, 0), (4, 6)$, and $(12, 6)$. Where do the diagonals of this parallelogram intersect?

(From Unit 6, Lesson 15.)

7. Lines ℓ and p are parallel. Select **all** true statements.

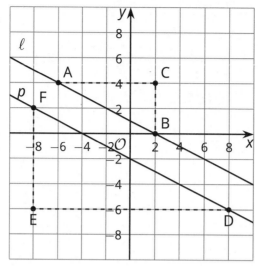

A. Triangle ADB is congruent to triangle CEF.

B. The slope of line ℓ is equal to the slope of line p.

C. Triangle ADB is similar to triangle CEF.

D. $\sin(A) = \sin(C)$

E. $\cos(B) = \sin(C)$

(From Unit 6, Lesson 10.)

8. Mai wrote a proof that triangle AED is congruent to triangle CEB. Mai's proof is incomplete. How can Mai fix her proof?

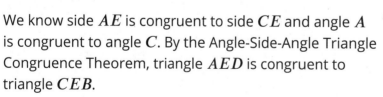

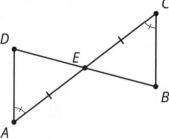

We know side AE is congruent to side CE and angle A is congruent to angle C. By the Angle-Side-Angle Triangle Congruence Theorem, triangle AED is congruent to triangle CEB.

(From Unit 2, Lesson 7.)

Lesson 2: Inscribed Angles

- Let's analyze angles made from chords.

2.1: Notice and Wonder: A New Angle

What do you notice? What do you wonder?

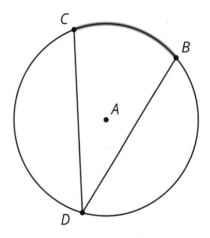

2.2: A Central Relationship

Here is a circle with central angle QAC.

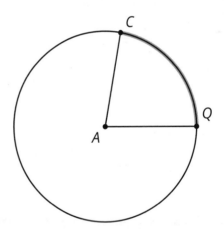

1. Use a protractor to find the approximate degree measure of angle QAC.

2. Mark a point B on the circle that is *not* on the highlighted arc from C to Q. Each member of your group should choose a different location for point B. Draw chords BC and BQ. Use a protractor to find the approximate degree measure of angle QBC.

3. Share your results with your group. What do you notice about your answers?

4. Make a conjecture about the relationship between an **inscribed angle** and the central angle that defines the same arc.

Are you ready for more?

Here is a special case of an inscribed angle where one of the chords that defines the inscribed angle goes through the center. The central angle DCF measures θ degrees, and the inscribed angle DEF measures α degrees. Prove that $\alpha = \frac{1}{2}\theta$.

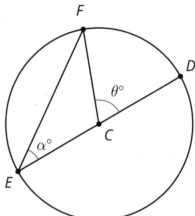

2.3: Similarity Returns

The image shows a circle with chords CD, CB, ED, and EB. The highlighted arc from point C to point E measures 100 degrees. The highlighted arc from point D to point B measures 140 degrees.

Prove that triangles CFD and EFB are similar.

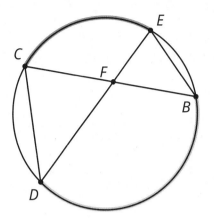

Lesson 2 Summary

We have discussed central angles such as angle AOB. Another kind of angle in a circle is an **inscribed angle**, or an angle formed by 2 chords that share an endpoint. In the image, angle ACB is an inscribed angle.

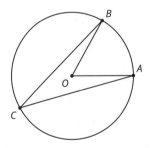

It looks as though the inscribed angle is smaller than the central angle that defines the same arc. In fact, the measure of an inscribed angle is always exactly half the measure of the associated central angle. For example, if the central angle AOB measures 50 degrees, the inscribed angle ACB must measure 25 degrees, even if we move point C along the circumference (without going past A or B). This also means that all inscribed angles that define the same arc are congruent.

Glossary
- inscribed angle

Lesson 2 Practice Problems

1. The measure of angle AOB is 56 degrees. What is the measure of angle ACB?

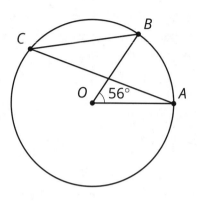

2. Explain the difference between central and inscribed angles.

3. What is the measure of the arc from A to B that does not pass through C?

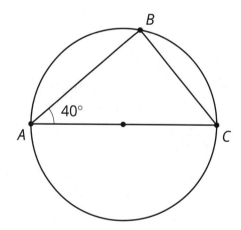

   A. 160 degrees

   B. 140 degrees

   C. 100 degrees

   D. 90 degrees

4. Find the values of x, y, and z.

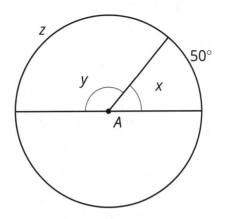

(From Unit 7, Lesson 1.)

5. Match the vocabulary term with the label.

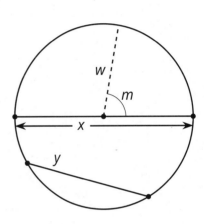

A. chord that is not a diameter   1. m

B. diameter   2. w

C. radius   3. x

D. central angle   4. y

(From Unit 7, Lesson 1.)

6. Triangle ABC has vertices at $(-4, 0)$, $(-2, 12)$, and $(12, 0)$. What is the point of intersection of its medians?

   A. $(4, 0)$

   B. $(5, 6)$

   C. $(2, 4)$

   D. $(4, 2)$

(From Unit 6, Lesson 16.)

7. The rule $(x, y) \rightarrow (y, -x)$ takes a line to a perpendicular line. Select another rule that takes a line to a perpendicular line.

   A. $(x, y) \rightarrow (-y, -x)$

   B. $(x, y) \rightarrow (2y, 2x)$

   C. $(x, y) \rightarrow (-4y, 4x)$

   D. $(x, y) \rightarrow (0.25y, -4)$

(From Unit 6, Lesson 11.)

Lesson 3: Tangent Lines

- Let's explore lines that intersect a circle in exactly 1 point.

3.1: Swim to Shore

Line ℓ represents a straight part of the shoreline at a beach. Suppose you are in the ocean at point C and you want to get to the shore as fast as possible. Assume there is no current. Segments CJ and CD represent 2 possible paths.

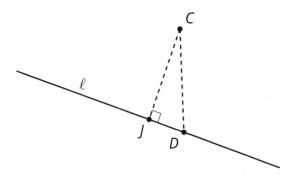

Diego says, "No matter where we put point D, the Pythagorean Theorem tells us that segment CJ is shorter than segment CD. So, segment CJ represents the shortest path to shore."

Do you agree with Diego? Explain your reasoning.

3.2: A Particular Perpendicular

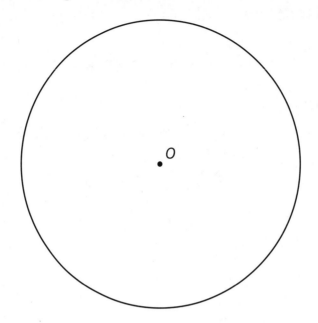

1. Draw a radius in the circle. Mark the point where the radius intersects the circle and label it A.

2. Construct a line perpendicular to the radius that goes through point A. Label this line n.

3. Line n intersects the circle in exactly 1 point, A. Why is it impossible for line n to intersect the circle in more than 1 point?

4. What kind of line, then, is n?

Geometry iM KH

Are you ready for more?

Here is a circle centered at O with radius 1 unit. Line AB is tangent to the circle.

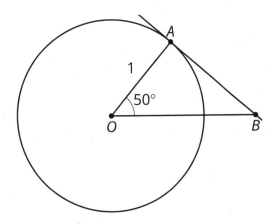

1. Calculate the length of segment AB.

2. How does the length of segment AB relate to the tangent of 50 degrees? Why is this true?

3. In right triangle trigonometry, "tangent" is defined in terms of side ratios. Write another definition of tangent (in the sense of a numerical value, not a line) in terms of a circle with radius 1 unit.

3.3: Another Angle

The image shows an angle whose rays are **tangent** to a circle.

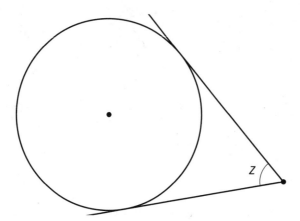

1. Mark the approximate points of tangency.

2. Draw the 2 radii that intersect these points of tangency. Label the measure of the central angle that is formed w.

3. What is the value of $w + z$? Explain or show your reasoning.

Lesson 3 Summary

A line is said to be **tangent** to a circle if it intersects the circle in exactly 1 point. Suppose line ℓ is tangent to a circle centered at A. Draw a radius from the center of the circle to the point of tangency, or the point where line ℓ intersects the circle. Call this point B. It looks like radius AB is perpendicular to line ℓ. Can we prove it?

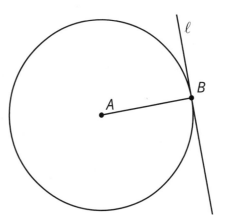

Every other point on the tangent line is outside the circle, so they must all be further away from the center than the point where the tangent intersects. This means the point B where the tangent line intersects the circle is the closest point on the line to the center point A. The radius AB must be perpendicular to the tangent line because the shortest distance from a point to a line is always along a perpendicular path.

Glossary

- tangent (line)

Lesson 3 Practice Problems

1. Line BD is tangent to a circle with diameter AB. Explain why the measure of angle BCA must equal the measure of angle ABD.

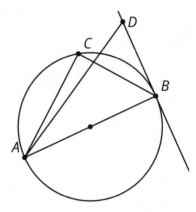

2. Line AC is perpendicular to the circle centered at O with radius 1 unit. The length of AC is 1.5 units. Find the length of segment AB.

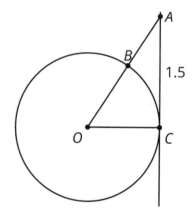

3. *Technology required.* Line PD is tangent to a circle of radius 1 inch centered at O. The length of PD is 1.2 inches. The length of AB is 1.7 inches. Which point on the circle is closest to point P?

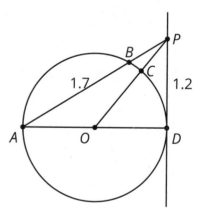

   A. point A

   B. point B

   C. point C

   D. point D

4. The arc from A to B not passing through C measures 50 degrees. Select **all** the true statements.

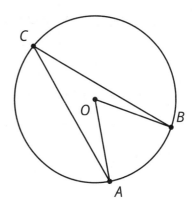

    A. Angle BCA measures 50 degrees.

    B. Angle BCA measures 25 degrees.

    C. Angle BOA measures 50 degrees.

    D. The arc from B to C not passing through A measures 180 degrees.

    E. Angles CBO and CAO are congruent.

(From Unit 7, Lesson 2.)

5. Chords AC and DB intersect at point E. List 3 pairs of angles that *must* be congruent.

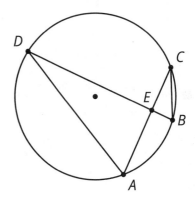

(From Unit 7, Lesson 2.)

6. The image shows a circle with diameters AC and BD. Prove that chords BC and AD (not drawn) are congruent.

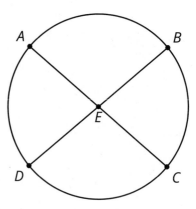

(From Unit 7, Lesson 1.)

7. The line represented by $y + 3 = -3(x + 6)$ is transformed by the rule $(x, y) \rightarrow (-x, -y)$. What is the slope of the image?

A. 3

B. $\frac{1}{3}$

C. $-\frac{1}{3}$

D. -3

(From Unit 6, Lesson 12.)

Lesson 4: Quadrilaterals in Circles

- Let's investigate quadrilaterals that fit in a circle.

4.1: Connecting the Dots

For each quadrilateral, use a compass to see if you can draw a circle that passes through all 4 of the quadrilateral's vertices.

A

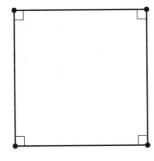

B

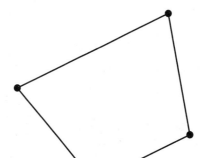

C

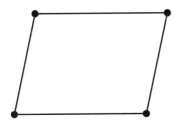

4.2: Inscribed Angles and Circumscribed Circles

1. The images show 3 quadrilaterals with **circumscribed** circles.

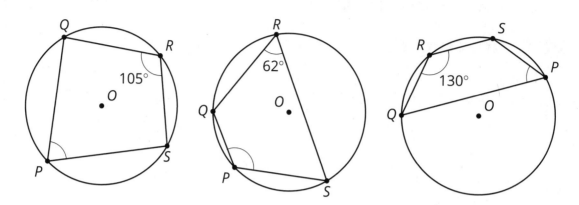

A   B   C

For each one, highlight the arc from S to Q passing through P. Then, find the measures of:

    a. the arc you highlighted

    b. the other arc from S to Q

    c. angle SPQ

2. Here is another quadrilateral with a circumscribed circle. What is the value of $\alpha + \beta$? Explain or show your reasoning.

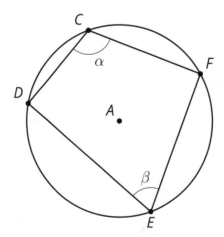

Are you ready for more?

Brahmagupta's formula states that for a quadrilateral whose vertices all lie on the same circle, the area of the quadrilateral is $\sqrt{(s-a)(s-b)(s-c)(s-d)}$ where $a, b, c,$ and d are the lengths of the quadrilateral's sides and s is half its perimeter.

In the cyclic quadrilateral in the image, point O is the center of the quadrilateral's circumscribed circle. Validate Brahmagupta's formula for this particular quadrilateral by first finding the sum of the areas of the top and bottom triangles. Then, calculate the area again using Brahmagupta's formula.

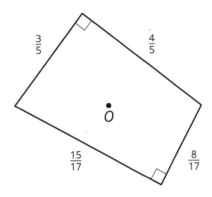

4.3: Construction Ahead

Quadrilateral $ABCD$ is a **cyclic quadrilateral**.

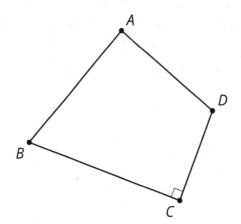

1. Draw diagonal BD. How will this diagonal relate to the circumscribed circle? Explain your reasoning.

2. Construct the center of the circumscribed circle for quadrilateral $ABCD$. Label this point O. Explain why your method worked.

3. Construct the circumscribed circle for quadrilateral $ABCD$.

4. Could we follow this procedure to construct a circumscribed circle for *any* cyclic quadrilaterals? Explain your reasoning.

Lesson 4 Summary

A circle is said to be **circumscribed** about a polygon if all the vertices of the polygon lie on the circle. If it is possible to draw a circumscribed circle for a quadrilateral, the figure is called a **cyclic quadrilateral**. Not all quadrilaterals have this property.

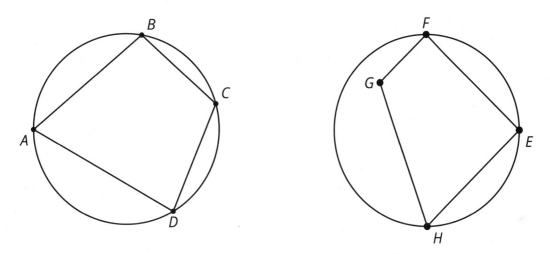

We can prove that the opposite angles of a cyclic quadrilateral are supplementary. Consider opposite angles BCD and BAD, labeled α and β.

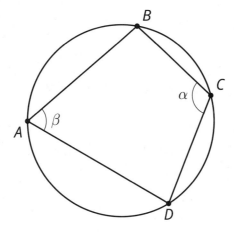

Angle BAD is inscribed in the arc from B to D through C. Angle BCD is inscribed in the arc from B to D through A. Together, the 2 arcs trace out the entire circumference of the circle, so their measures add to 360 degrees. By the Inscribed Angle Theorem, the sum of α and β must be half of 360 degrees, or 180 degrees. So angles BAD and BCD are supplementary. The same argument can be applied to the other pair of opposite angles.

Glossary

- circumscribed
- cyclic quadrilateral

Lesson 4 Practice Problems

1. A quadrilateral $ABCD$ has the given angle measures. Select **all** measurements which could come from a cyclic quadrilateral.

    A. angle A is 90°, angle B is 90°, angle C is 90°, and angle D is 90°

    B. angle A is 80°, angle B is 80°, angle C is 100°, and angle D is 100°

    C. angle A is 70°, angle B is 110°, angle C is 70°, and angle D is 110°

    D. angle A is 60°, angle B is 50°, angle C is 120°, and angle D is 130°

    E. angle A is 50°, angle B is 40°, angle C is 120°, and angle D is 150°

2. Quadrilateral $ABCD$ is cyclic with given angle measures.

    a. What is the measure of angle C?

    b. What is the measure of angle D?

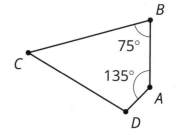

3. Lin is looking at cyclic quadrilateral $ABCD$. She says, "I'm not convinced that opposite angles of cyclic quadrilaterals always add up to 180 degrees. For example, in this diagram, suppose we moved point A to a different spot on the circle. Angle BCD would still measure 100 degrees, but now angle BAD would have a different measure, and they wouldn't add up to 180."

    Do you agree with Lin? Explain or show your reasoning.

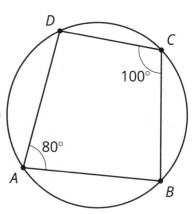

4. Line AC is tangent to the circle centered at O with radius 3 units. The length of segment AC is 4.5 units. Find the length of segment AB.

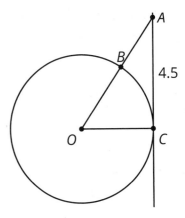

A. $3 + \sqrt{29.25}$ units

B. $\sqrt{29.25}$ units

C. $-3 + \sqrt{29.25}$ units

D. 26.25 units

(From Unit 7, Lesson 3.)

5. *Technology required.* Line PD is tangent to a circle of radius 1 inch centered at O. The length of segment PD is 1.2 inches. The length of segment AB is 1.7 inches. Han is trying to figure out if C or B is closer to P. He uses the Pythagorean Theorem to find the length of OP. Then he subtracts 1 from the length of OP to determine how far C is from point P.

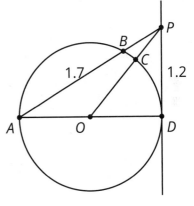

a. How far is B from point P?

b. Which point is closest to P? Explain your reasoning.

(From Unit 7, Lesson 3.)

6. In the diagram, the measure of angle ACB is 25 degrees. What is the measure of angle AOB?

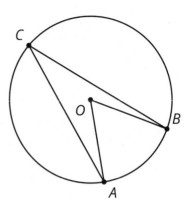

(From Unit 7, Lesson 2.)

7. Which statement **must** be true?

   A. A diameter is a chord.

   B. A chord is a radius.

   C. A chord is a diameter.

   D. A central angle's vertex is on the circle.

(From Unit 7, Lesson 1.)

8. A circle and line are drawn. How many intersection points are possible? Select **all** possible answers.

   A. 0

   B. 1

   C. 2

   D. 3

   E. 4

(From Unit 6, Lesson 13.)

Lesson 5: Triangles in Circles

- Let's see how perpendicular bisectors relate to circumscribed circles.

5.1: One Perpendicular Bisector

The image shows a triangle.

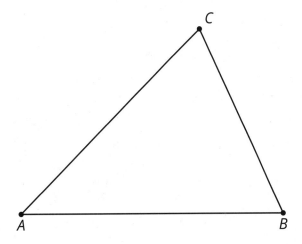

1. Construct the perpendicular bisector of segment AB.

2. Imagine a point D placed anywhere on the perpendicular bisector you constructed. How would the distance from D to A compare to the distance from D to B? Explain your reasoning.

5.2: Three Perpendicular Bisectors

1. Construct the perpendicular bisector of segment BC from the earlier activity. Label the point where the 2 perpendicular bisectors intersect as P.

2. Use a colored pencil to draw segments PA, PB, and PC. How do the lengths of these segments compare? Explain your reasoning.

3. Imagine the perpendicular bisector of segment AC. Will it pass through point P? Explain your reasoning.

4. Construct the perpendicular bisector of segment AC.

5. Construct a circle centered at P with radius PA.

6. Why does the circle also pass through points B and C?

Are you ready for more?

Points A, B, and C are graphed. Find the coordinates of the circumcenter and the radius of the circumscribed circle for triangle ABC.

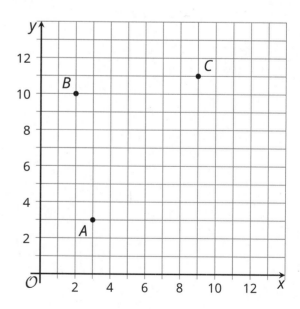

5.3: Wandering Centers

Each student in your group should choose 1 triangle. It's okay for 2 students to choose the same triangle as long as all 3 are chosen by at least 1 student.

1. Construct the circumscribed circle of your triangle.

2. After you finish, compare your results. What do you notice about the location of the **circumcenter** in each triangle?

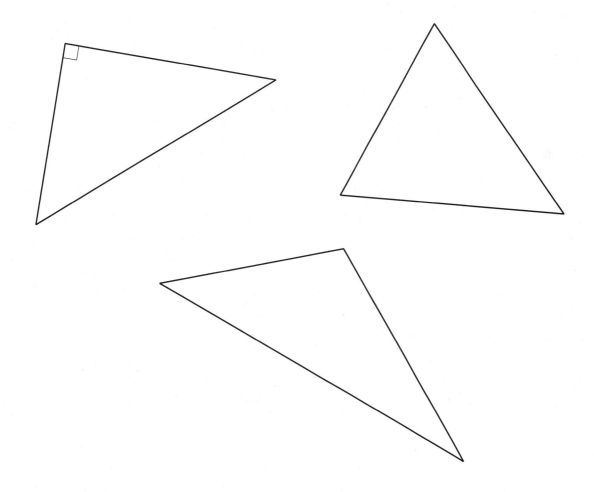

Lesson 5 Summary

We saw that some quadrilaterals have circumscribed circles. Is the same true for triangles? In fact, *all* triangles have circumscribed circles. The key fact is that all points on the perpendicular bisector of a segment are equidistant from the endpoints of the segment.

Suppose we have triangle ABC and we construct the perpendicular bisectors of all 3 sides. These perpendicular bisectors will all meet at a single point called the **circumcenter** of the triangle (label it D). This point is on the perpendicular bisector of AB, so it's equidistant from A and B. It's also on the perpendicular bisector of BC, so it's equidistant from B and C. So, it is actually the same distance from A, B, *and* C. We can draw a circle centered at D with radius AD. The circle will pass through B and C too because the distances BD and CD are the same as the radius of the circle.

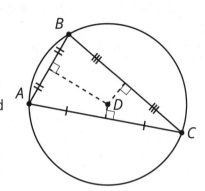

In this case, the circumcenter happened to fall inside triangle ABC, but that does not need to happen. The images show cases where the circumcenter is inside a triangle, outside a triangle, and on one of the sides of a triangle.

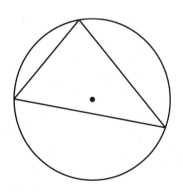 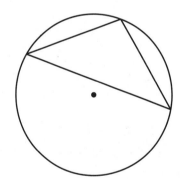 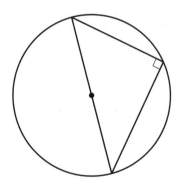

Glossary

- circumcenter

Geometry iM KH

Lesson 5 Practice Problems

1. Noah says, "I constructed 2 perpendicular bisectors of triangle ABC. That means the point where they intersect is the circumcenter!" Andre responds, "No, we still need to check the third perpendicular bisector to make sure it intersects at the same point."

   Do you agree with either of them? Explain or show your reasoning.

2. The dotted line is the perpendicular bisector of side AB. The distance between points E and A is 7 units. What is the distance between points E and B? Explain or show your reasoning.

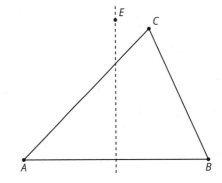

3. Construct the circumcenter of each triangle. Then, based on the locations of the circumcenters, classify each triangle as acute, right, or obtuse.

   triangle A

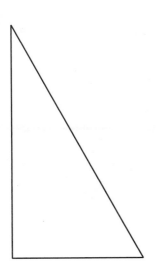

   triangle B

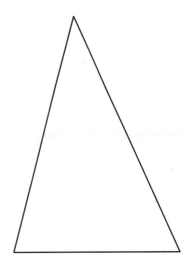

4. Select **all** quadrilaterals that **cannot** be cyclic.

A. a square with side length $\sqrt{5}$ units

B. a 2 inch by 4 inch rectangle

C. a rhombus with side length 5 centimeters and angle measures 20 degrees and 160 degrees

D. quadrilateral $ABCD$ in which angle A is 62 degrees, angle B is 97 degrees, angle C is 118 degrees, and angle D is 83 degrees

E. quadrilateral $WXYZ$ in which angle W is 45 degrees, angle X is 135 degrees, angle Y is 90 degrees, and angle Z is 90 degrees

(From Unit 7, Lesson 4.)

5. A quadrilateral $ABCD$ has the given angle measures. Select the set of measurements which could come from a cyclic quadrilateral.

A. angle A is 70°, angle B is 110°, angle C is 70°, and angle D is 110°

B. angle A is 60°, angle B is 50°, angle C is 120°, and angle D is 130°

C. angle A is 100°, angle B is 110°, angle C is 70°, and angle D is 80°

D. angle A is 70°, angle B is 45°, angle C is 110°, and angle D is 45°

(From Unit 7, Lesson 4.)

6. What is the measure of angle YXZ?

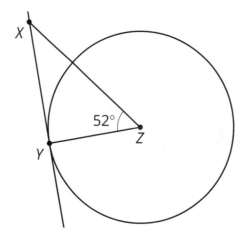

(From Unit 7, Lesson 3.)

7. The measure of angle AOB is 56 degrees.

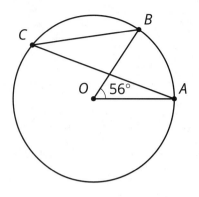

    a. What is the measure of angle ACB?

    b. What is the measure of the arc from A to B not passing through C?

(From Unit 7, Lesson 2.)

8. A quadrilateral has vertices $A = (0, 0)$, $B = (2, 4)$, $C = (0, 5)$, and $D = (-2, 1)$. Select the most precise classification for quadrilateral $ABCD$.

    A. quadrilateral

    B. parallelogram

    C. rectangle

    D. square

(From Unit 6, Lesson 14.)

Lesson 6: A Special Point

- Let's see what we can learn about a triangle by watching how salt piles up on it.

6.1: Notice and Wonder: Salt Pile

What do you notice? What do you wonder?

6.2: Point and Angle

Here is an angle BAC with 2 different sets of markings.

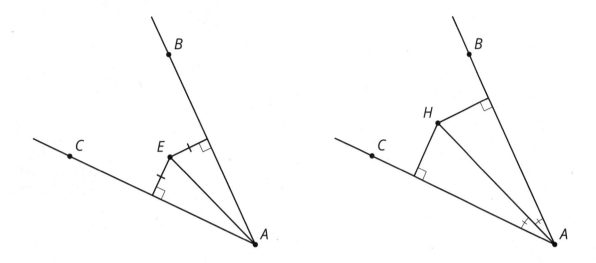

1. Point E is the same distance away from each of the 2 rays that form angle BAC. Make a conjecture about angles EAB and EAC and prove it.

2. Point H is on the angle bisector of angle BAC. What can you prove about the distances from H to each ray?

6.3: What If There Are Three Sides?

Two angle bisectors have been constructed in triangle ABC. They intersect at point G.

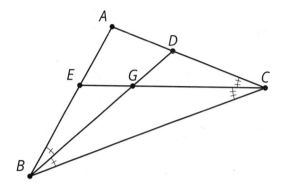

1. Sketch segments that show the distances from point G to each side of the triangle.

2. How do the distances from point G to sides AB and BC compare? Explain your reasoning.

3. How do the distances from point G to sides AC and BC compare? Explain your reasoning.

4. Will the third angle bisector pass through point G? Explain your reasoning.

Are you ready for more?

What shape would the ridge form if you poured salt onto a piece of cardboard with a long straight edge and a small hole cut out of it? Explain your reasoning.

Lesson 6 Summary

Salt piles up in an interesting way when poured onto a triangle. Why does that happen?

As the salt piles up and reaches a maximum height, new grains of salt will fall off toward whichever side of the triangle is closest. We can show that points on an angle bisector are equidistant from the rays that form the angle. So, salt grains that land on an angle bisector will balance and not fall towards either side. This is why we see ridges form in the salt.

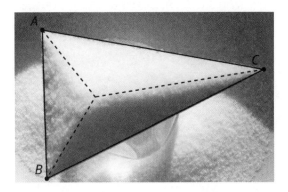

As we might conjecture from the salt example, all 3 angle bisectors in a triangle meet at a single point, called the triangle's **incenter**. To see why this is true, consider any 2 angle bisectors in a triangle. The point where they meet is the same distance from the first and second sides, and also the same distance from the second and third sides. Therefore, it's the same distance from *all* sides, so the third angle bisector must also go through this point.

In the images, segments RT, AD, BD, and CD are angle bisectors. This means that point T is the same distance from ray RQ as it is from ray RS. In triangle ABC, point D is the same distance from all 3 sides of the triangle—it's the triangle's incenter.

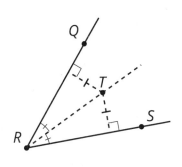

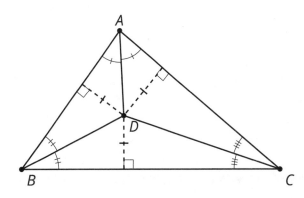

Glossary

- incenter

Lesson 6 Practice Problems

1. How do the values of α and β compare? Explain your reasoning.

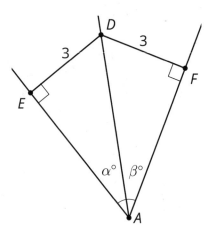

2. Triangle ABC is shown together with its angle bisectors. Draw a point D that is equidistant from sides AC and BC, but which is closest to side AB.

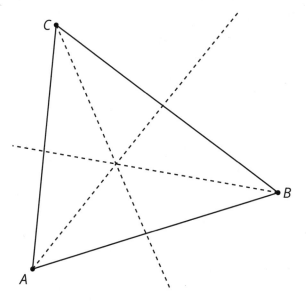

3. In triangle ABC, point D is the incenter. Sketch segments to represent the distance from point D to the sides of the triangle. How must these distances compare?

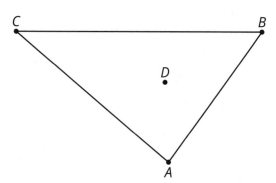

Geometry iM KH

4. Triangle ABC has circumcenter D.

    a. Sketch the 3 lines that intersect at the circumcenter.

    b. If the distance from point D to point A is 5 units, what is the distance from point D to point C? Explain or show your reasoning.

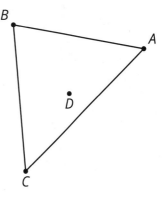

(From Unit 7, Lesson 5.)

5. The angles of triangle ABC measure 50 degrees, 40 degrees, and 90 degrees. Will its circumcenter fall inside the triangle, on the triangle, or outside the triangle?

    A. inside the triangle

    B. on the triangle

    C. outside the triangle

(From Unit 7, Lesson 5.)

6. Tyler and Kiran are discussing the parallelogram in the image. Tyler says the parallelogram cannot be cyclic. Kiran says the parallelogram can be cyclic if a circle is drawn carefully through the vertices.

Do you agree with either of them? Explain or show your reasoning.

(From Unit 7, Lesson 4.)

7. Find the measures of the remaining angles of quadrilateral $WXYZ$.

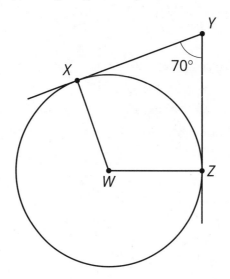

(From Unit 7, Lesson 3.)

8. Which expression describes a point that partitions a segment AB in a 1 : 5 ratio?

A. $\frac{1}{5}A + \frac{4}{5}B$

B. $\frac{1}{6}A + \frac{5}{6}B$

C. $\frac{4}{5}A + \frac{1}{5}B$

D. $\frac{5}{6}A + \frac{1}{6}B$

(From Unit 6, Lesson 15.)

9. Write 3 expressions that can be used to find angle C.

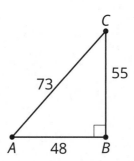

(From Unit 4, Lesson 9.)

Lesson 7: Circles in Triangles

- Let's construct the largest possible circle inside of a triangle.

7.1: The Largest Circle

Use a compass to draw the largest circle you can find that fits inside each triangle.

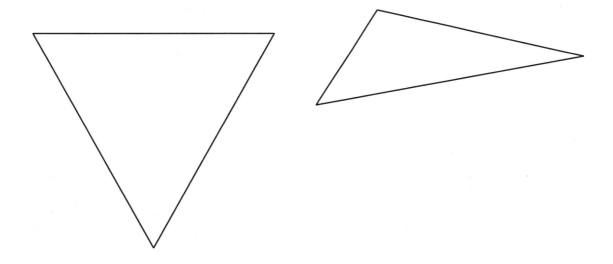

7.2: The Inner Circle

1. Mark 3 points and connect them with a straightedge to make a large triangle. The triangle should *not* be equilateral.

2. Construct the incenter of the triangle.

3. Construct the segments that show the distance from the incenter to the sides of the triangle.

4. Construct a circle centered at the incenter using one of the segments you just constructed as a radius.

5. Would it matter which of the three segments you use? Explain your thinking.

7.3: Equilateral Centers

The image shows an equilateral triangle ABC. The angle bisectors are drawn. The incenter is plotted and labeled D.

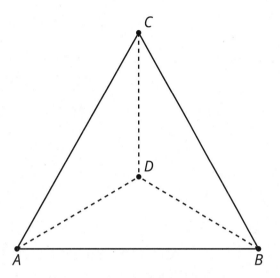

Prove that the incenter is also the circumcenter.

Are you ready for more?

1. Suppose we have an equilateral triangle. Find the ratio of the area of the triangle's circumscribed circle to the area of its inscribed circle.

2. Is this ratio the same for all triangles? Explain or show your reasoning.

Lesson 7 Summary

We have seen that the incenter of a triangle is the same distance from all 3 sides of the triangle. If we draw the congruent segments representing the distance from the incenter to the triangle's sides, we can think of them as radii of a circle centered at the incenter. This circle is the triangle's inscribed circle.

In this diagram, segments BD, CD, and AD are angle bisectors. Point D is the triangle's incenter, and the circle is inscribed in the triangle.

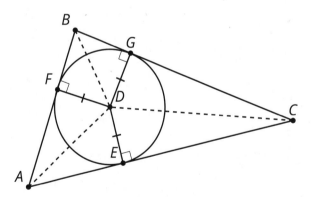

The inscribed circle is the largest possible circle that can be drawn inside a triangle. Also, the 3 radii that represent the distances from the incenter to the sides of the triangle are by definition perpendicular to the sides of the triangle. This means the circle is tangent to all 3 sides of the triangle.

Lesson 7 Practice Problems

1. Triangle ABC is shown with its incenter at D. The inscribed circle's radius measures 2 units. The length of AB is 9 units. The length of BC is 10 units. The length of AC is 17 units.

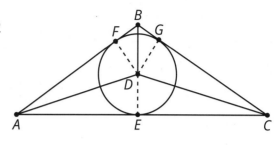

    a. What is the area of triangle ACD?

    b. What is the area of triangle ABC?

2. Triangle ABC is shown with an inscribed circle of radius 4 units centered at point D. The inscribed circle is tangent to side AB at the point G. The length of AG is 6 units and the length of BG is 8 units. What is the measure of angle A?

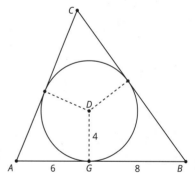

    A. $\arctan\left(\frac{2}{3}\right)$

    B. $2\arctan\left(\frac{2}{3}\right)$

    C. $\arcsin\left(\frac{2}{3}\right)$

    D. $2\arccos\left(\frac{2}{3}\right)$

3. Construct the inscribed circle for the triangle.

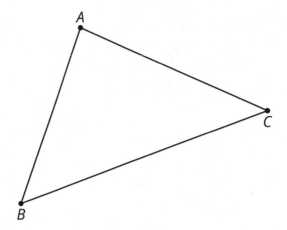

4. Point D lies on the angle bisector of angle ACB. Point E lies on the perpendicular bisector of side AB.

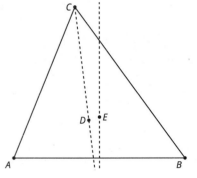

   a. What can we say about the distance between point D and the sides and vertices of triangle ABC?

   b. What can we say about the distance between point E and the sides and vertices of triangle ABC?

(From Unit 7, Lesson 6.)

5. Construct the incenter of the triangle. Explain your reasoning.

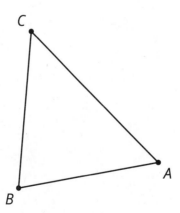

(From Unit 7, Lesson 6.)

6. The angles of triangle ABC measure 30 degrees, 40 degrees, and 110 degrees. Will its circumcenter fall inside the triangle, on the triangle, or outside the triangle? Explain your reasoning.

(From Unit 7, Lesson 5.)

7. The images show 2 possible blueprints for a park. The park planners want to build a water fountain that is equidistant from each of the corners of the park. Is this possible for either park? Explain or show your reasoning.

park A   **park B**

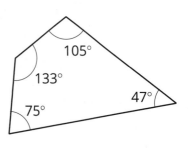

(From Unit 7, Lesson 4.)

8. Triangle ABC has vertices at $(-8, 2), (2, 6),$ and $(10, 2)$. What is the point of intersection of the triangle's medians?

(From Unit 6, Lesson 16.)

Lesson 8: Arcs and Sectors

- Let's analyze portions of circles.

8.1: Math Talk: Fractions of a Circle

Evaluate each problem mentally.

- Find the area of the shaded portion of the circle.

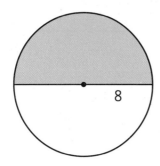

- Find the length of the highlighted portion of the circle's circumference.

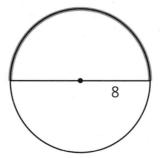

- Find the area of the shaded portion of the circle.

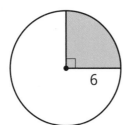

- Find the length of the highlighted portion of the circle's circumference.

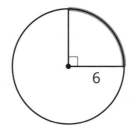

Geometry iM KH

8.2: Sector Areas and Arc Lengths

A **sector** of a circle is the region enclosed by 2 radii.

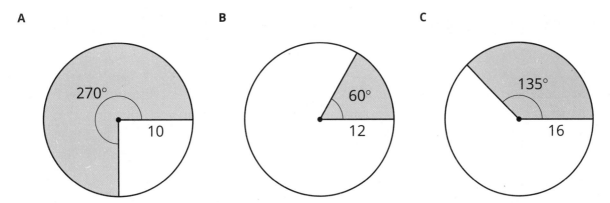

For each circle, find the area of the shaded sector and the length of the arc that outlines the sector. All units are centimeters. Give your answers in terms of π.

Are you ready for more?

1. What length of rope would you need to wrap around Earth's equator exactly once?

2. Suppose you lengthen the rope, then suspend it so it is an equal distance away from Earth at all points around the equator. How much rope would you have to add in order to allow a person to walk underneath it?

3. What length of rope would you need to wrap around the circumference of a hula hoop with radius 70 centimeters exactly once?

4. Suppose you lengthen the rope, then lay the hula hoop and the rope on the floor, with the rope arranged in a circle with the same center as the hula hoop. How much rope would you have to add in order to allow a person to lie down on the floor with their toes pointing towards the hula hoop and their head towards the rope, but touching neither?

8.3: Build a Method

Mai says, "I know how to find the area of a sector or the length of an arc for central angles like 180 degrees or 90 degrees. But I don't know how to do it for central angles that make up more complicated fractions of the circle."

1. In the diagram, the sector's central angle measures θ degrees and the circle's radius is r units. Use the diagram to tell Mai how to find the *area of a sector* and the *length of an arc* for any angle and radius measure.

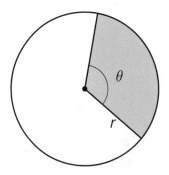

2. This image shows a circle with radius and central angle measurements. Find the area of the shaded sector, and the length of the arc defined by the sector.

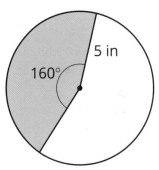

Lesson 8 Summary

A **sector** of a circle is the region enclosed by 2 radii. To find the area of a sector, start by calculating the area of the whole circle. Divide the measure of the central angle of the sector by 360 to find the fraction of the circle represented by the sector. Then, multiply this fraction by the circle's total area. We can use a similar process to find the length of the arc lying on the boundary of the sector.

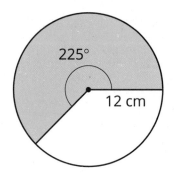

The circle in the image has a total area of 144π square centimeters, and its circumference is 24π centimeters. To find the area of the sector with a 225° central angle, divide 225 by 360 to get $\frac{5}{8}$ or 0.625. Multiply this by 144π to find that the area of the sector is 90π square centimeters. The length of the arc defined by the sector is 15π because $24\pi \cdot \frac{5}{8} = 15\pi$.

Glossary

- sector

Geometry iM KH

Lesson 8 Practice Problems

1. Suppose a circle is divided into congruent slices. Match each number of slices with the resulting central angle measure of each slice.

A. 2		1. 45°	
B. 3		2. 60°	
C. 4		3. 72°	
D. 5		4. 120°	
E. 6		5. 90°	
F. 8		6. 180°	

2. A circle of radius 12 units is divided into 8 congruent slices.

    a. What is the area of each slice?

    b. What is the arc length of each slice?

3. Diego says, "To find arc length, divide the measure of the central angle by 360. Then multiply that by the area of the circle." Do you agree with Diego? Show or explain your reasoning.

4. The image shows a triangle.

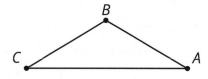

a. Sketch the inscribed and circumscribed circles for this triangle.

b. Compare and contrast the 2 circles.

(From Unit 7, Lesson 7.)

5. Triangle ABC is shown with its inscribed circle drawn. The measure of angle ECF is 72 degrees. What is the measure of angle EGF? Explain or show your reasoning.

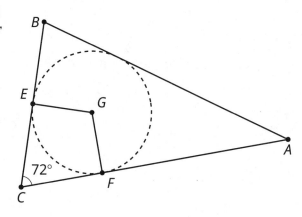

(From Unit 7, Lesson 7.)

6. How do the values of x and y compare? Explain your reasoning.

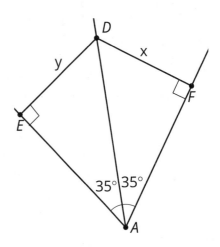

(From Unit 7, Lesson 6.)

7. Points A, B, and C are the corners of a triangular park. The park district is going to add a set of swings inside the park. The goal is to have the swings equidistant from the vertices of the park. Find a location that meets this goal. Explain or show your reasoning.

B

A

C

(From Unit 7, Lesson 5.)

8. In the diagram, the measure of the arc from A to B not passing through C is 80 degrees. What is the measure of angle ACB?

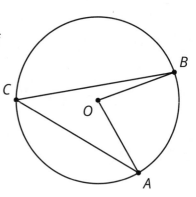

A. 20 degrees

B. 40 degrees

C. 80 degrees

D. 160 degrees

(From Unit 7, Lesson 2.)

9. This solid has curved sides. All cross sections parallel to the base are squares measuring 3 units on each side. The height from the base to the top is 8 units. What is the volume of this solid?

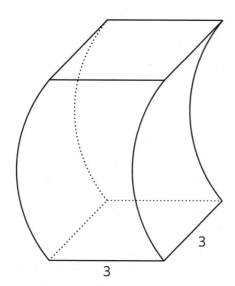

(From Unit 5, Lesson 10.)

Lesson 9: Part to Whole

- Let's see what we can figure out about a circle if we're given information about a sector of the circle.

9.1: What's Your Angle?

A circle has radius 10 centimeters. Suppose an arc on the circle has length π centimeters. What is the measure of the central angle whose radii define the arc?

9.2: Enough Information?

The central angle of this shaded sector measures 45 degrees, and the sector's area is 32π square inches.

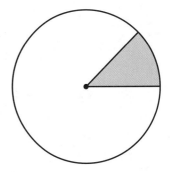

Kiran says, "We can find the area of the whole circle, the arc length of the sector, and the circumference of the circle with this information."

Priya says, "But how? We don't know the circle's radius!"

Do you agree with either of them? Explain or show your reasoning. Calculate as many of the values Kiran mentioned as possible.

Are you ready for more?

A Greek mathematician named Eratosthenes calculated the circumference of Earth more than 2,000 years ago. He used information similar to what is given here:

Seattle and San Francisco are on the same longitude line and 680 miles apart. At noon on a summer day, an upright meter stick in Seattle casts a shadow with an angle of 2 degrees. On the same day at the same time, an upright meter stick in San Francisco casts a shadow with an angle of 7.83 degrees.

image not to scale

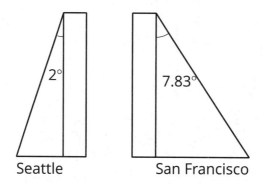

Use this information to calculate the circumference of Earth. Explain or show your reasoning.

9.3: Info Gap: From Sector to Circle

Your teacher will give you either a problem card or a data card. Do not show or read your card to your partner.

If your teacher gives you the data card:

1. Silently read the information on your card.

2. Ask your partner, "What specific information do you need?" and wait for your partner to ask for information. Only give information that is on your card. (Do not figure out anything for your partner!)

3. Before telling your partner the information, ask, "Why do you need to know (that piece of information)?"

4. Read the problem card, and solve the problem independently.

5. Share the data card, and discuss your reasoning.

If your teacher gives you the problem card:

1. Silently read your card and think about what information you need to answer the question.

2. Ask your partner for the specific information that you need.

3. Explain to your partner how you are using the information to solve the problem.

4. When you have enough information, share the problem card with your partner, and solve the problem independently.

5. Read the data card, and discuss your reasoning.

Pause here so your teacher can review your work. Ask your teacher for a new set of cards and repeat the activity, trading roles with your partner.

Lesson 9 Summary

We can work backward from information about a sector or arc to get information about the whole circle.

Suppose a circle has an arc with length 7π units that is defined by a 90 degree central angle. This arc makes up $\frac{1}{4}$ of the entire circumference of the circle because $360 \div 90 = 4$. So, we can multiply the arc's length by 4 to find that the entire circumference measures 28π units. The circumference of a circle can be calculated using the expression $2\pi r$, so we know that $2\pi r = 28\pi$. The value of r must be 14 units.

For more difficult problems, we can write equations. Suppose a circle has a sector with area 135π square units and a central angle of 216 degrees. Let x stand for the area of the whole circle. Dividing 216 by 360 gives the fraction of the circle represented by the sector. Multiply that fraction by x and set it equal to the area of the sector.

$$\frac{216}{360}x = 135\pi$$

Solve this equation to find that the circle's area is 225π square units. This tells us that $\pi r^2 = 225\pi$. The value of r must be the positive number that squares to make 225, or 15 units.

Geometry iM KH

Lesson 9 Practice Problems

1. Jada cuts out a rectangular piece of paper that measures 5 inches by 4 inches. Han cuts out a paper sector of a circle with radius 5 inches, and calculates the arc length to be 2π inches. Whose paper is larger? Show your reasoning.

2. A circle has radius 10 centimeters. Suppose an arc on the circle has length 8π centimeters. What is the measure of the central angle whose radii define the arc?

3. A circle has radius 6 units. For each arc length, find the area of a sector of this circle which defines that arc length.

   a. 4π units

   b. 5π units

   c. 10 units

   d. ℓ units

4. Select **all** the sectors which have an area of 3π square units.

   A. a sector with a radius of 6 units and a central angle of 30 degrees

   B. a sector with a radius of 6 units and a central angle of 45 degrees

   C. a sector with a radius of 3 units and a central angle of 60 degrees

   D. a sector with a radius of 3 units and a central angle of 120 degrees

   E. a sector with a radius of 3 units and a central angle of 180 degrees

   (From Unit 7, Lesson 8.)

5. A circle has radius 4 units and a central angle measuring 45 degrees. What is the length of the arc defined by the central angle?

(From Unit 7, Lesson 8.)

6. Clare and Diego are discussing inscribing circles in quadrilaterals.

Diego thinks that you can inscribe a circle in *any* quadrilateral since you can inscribe a circle in any triangle. Clare thinks it is not always possible because she does not think the angle bisectors are guaranteed to intersect at a single point. She claims she can draw a quadrilateral for which an inscribed circle can't be drawn.

Do you agree with either of them? Explain or show your reasoning.

(From Unit 7, Lesson 7.)

7. Triangle ABC is shown together with the angle bisectors of each of its angles. Draw a point D that is equidistant from sides AC and AB, but which is closest to side BC.

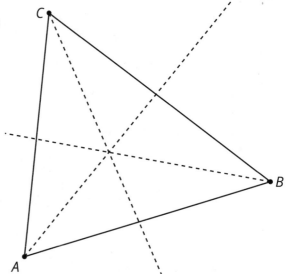

(From Unit 7, Lesson 6.)

Geometry **iM KH**

8. Priya and Mai are trying to prove that if 2 chords are congruent, they are equidistant from the center of the circle. Priya draws this picture.

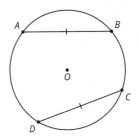

Mai adds the perpendicular segment from the center of the circle to each chord.

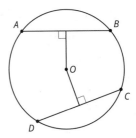

Priya says, "I think we should try to use triangles because that is how we proved things congruent before." Mai says, "I think you're right, but how? Should we draw in some radii?"

Help them complete the proof.

(From Unit 7, Lesson 1.)

Lesson 10: Angles, Arcs, and Radii

- Let's analyze relationships between arc lengths, radii, and central angles.

10.1: Comparing Progress

Han and Tyler are each completing the same set of tasks on an online homework site. Han is using his smartphone and Tyler is using his tablet computer. Their progress is indicated by the circular bars shown in the image. The shaded arc represents the tasks that have been completed. When the full circumference of the circle is shaded, they will be finished with all the tasks.

Han's progress

Tyler's progress

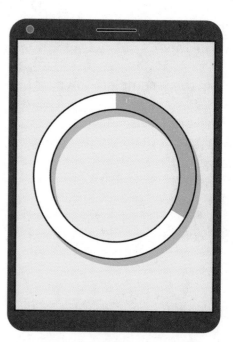

Tyler says, "The arc length on my progress bar measures 4.75 centimeters. The arc length on Han's progress bar measures 2.25 centimeters. So, I've completed more tasks than Han has."

1. Do you agree with Tyler? Why or why not?

2. What information would you need to make a completely accurate comparison between the two students' progress?

10.2: A Dilated Circle

The image shows 2 circles. The second circle is a dilation of the first circle using a scale factor of 3.

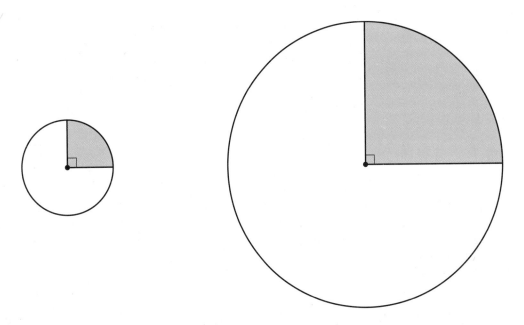

For each part of the dilated image, determine the factor by which it's changed when compared to the corresponding part of the original circle.

1. the area of the sector

2. the central angle of the sector

3. the radius

4. the length of the arc defined by the sector

5. the ratio of the circle's circumference to its diameter

10.3: Card Sort: Angles, Arcs, and Radii

Your teacher will give you a set of cards. Sort the cards into categories of your choosing. Be prepared to explain the meaning of your categories. Then, sort the cards into categories in a different way. Be prepared to explain the meaning of your new categories.

Are you ready for more?

For a circle of radius r, an expression that relates the area of a sector to the arc length defined by that sector is $\frac{1}{2}r\ell$ where ℓ is the length of the arc. Explain why this is true and provide an example.

Lesson 10 Summary

If we have the same central angle in 2 different circles, the length of the arc defined by the angle depends on the size of the circle. So, we can use the relationship between the arc length and the circle's radius to get some information about the size of the central angle.

For example, suppose circle A has radius 9 units and a central angle that defines an arc with length 3π. Circle B has radius 15 units and a central angle that defines an arc with length 5π. How do the 2 angles compare?

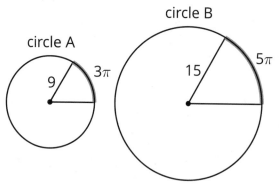

For the angle in Circle A, the ratio of the arc length to the radius is $\frac{3\pi}{9}$, which can be rewritten as $\frac{\pi}{3}$. For the angle in Circle B, the arc length to radius ratio is $\frac{5\pi}{15}$, which can also be written as $\frac{\pi}{3}$. That seems to indicate that the angles are the same size. Let's check.

Circle A's circumference is 18π units. The arc length 3π is $\frac{1}{6}$ of 18π, so the angle measurement must be $\frac{1}{6}$ of 360 degrees, or 60 degrees. Circle B's circumference is 30π units. The arc length 5π is $\frac{1}{6}$ of 30π, so this angle also measures $\frac{1}{6}$ of 360 degrees or 60 degrees. The 2 angles are indeed congruent.

Lesson 10 Practice Problems

1. Here are 2 circles. The smaller circle has radius r, circumference c, and diameter d. The larger circle has radius R, circumference C, and diameter D. The larger circle is a dilation of the smaller circle by a factor of k.

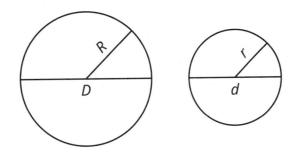

   Using the circles, write 3 pairs of equivalent ratios. Find the value of each set of ratios you wrote.

2. Tyler is confident that all circles are similar, but he cannot explain why this is true. Help Tyler explain why all circles are similar.

3. Circle B is a dilation of circle A.

circle A

circle B

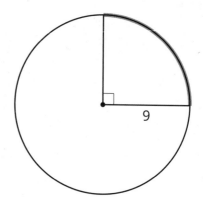

    a. What is the scale factor of dilation?

    b. What is the length of the highlighted arc in circle A?

    c. What is the length of the highlighted arc in circle B?

    d. What is the ratio of the arc lengths?

    e. How does the ratio of arc length compare to the scale factor?

4. Kiran cuts out a square piece of paper with side length 6 inches. Mai cuts out a paper sector of a circle with radius 6 inches, and calculates the arc length to be 4π inches. Whose paper is larger? Explain or show your reasoning.

(From Unit 7, Lesson 9.)

5. A circle has radius 3 centimeters. Suppose an arc on the circle has length 4π centimeters. What is the measure of the central angle whose radii define the arc?

(From Unit 7, Lesson 9.)

6. A circle with a shaded sector is shown.

   a. What is the area of the shaded sector?

   b. What is the length of the arc that outlines this sector?

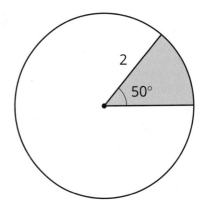

(From Unit 7, Lesson 8.)

7. The towns of Washington, Franklin, and Springfield are connected by straight roads. The towns wish to build an airport to be shared by all of them.

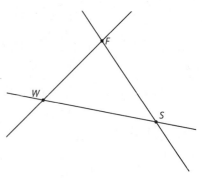

a. Where should they build the airport if they want it to be the same distance from each town's center? Describe how to find the precise location.

b. Where should they build the airport if they want it to be the same distance from each of the roads connecting the towns? Describe how to find the precise location.

(From Unit 7, Lesson 7.)

8. Chords AC and DB intersect at point E. Select **all** pairs of angles that must be congruent.

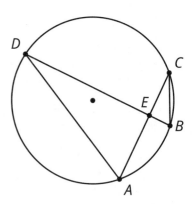

A. angle ADB and angle ACB

B. angle ADB and angle CAD

C. angle DEA and angle CEB

D. angle CAD and angle CBD

E. angle BCA and angle CBA

(From Unit 7, Lesson 2.)

Lesson 11: A New Way to Measure Angles

- Let's look at a new way to measure angles.

11.1: A One-Unit Radius

A circle has radius 1 unit. Find the length of the arc defined by each of these central angles. Give your answers in terms of π.

1. 180 degrees

2. 45 degrees

3. 270 degrees

4. 225 degrees

5. 360 degrees

11.2: A Constant Ratio

Diego and Lin are looking at 2 circles.

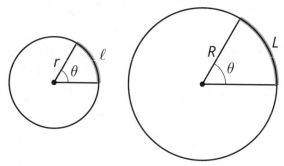

Diego says, "It seems like for a given central angle, the arc length is proportional to the radius. That is, the ratio $\frac{\ell}{r}$ has the same value as the ratio $\frac{L}{R}$ because they have the same central angle measure. Can we prove that this is true?"

Lin says, "The big circle is a dilation of the small circle. If k is the scale factor, then $R = kr$."

Diego says, "The arc length in the small circle is $\ell = \frac{\theta}{360} \cdot 2\pi r$. In the large circle, it's $L = \frac{\theta}{360} \cdot 2\pi R$. We can rewrite that as $L = \frac{\theta}{360} \cdot 2\pi rk$. So $L = k\ell$."

Lin says, "Okay, from here I can show that $\frac{\ell}{r}$ and $\frac{L}{R}$ are equivalent."

1. How does Lin know that the big circle is a dilation of the small circle?

2. How does Lin know that $R = kr$?

3. Why could Diego write $\ell = \frac{\theta}{360} \cdot 2\pi r$?

4. When Diego says that $L = k\ell$, what does that mean in words?

5. Why could Diego say that $L = k\ell$?

6. How can Lin show that $\frac{\ell}{r} = \frac{L}{R}$?

11.3: Defining Radians

Suppose we have a circle that has a central angle. The **radian** measure of the angle is the ratio of the length of the arc defined by the angle to the circle's radius. That is, $\theta = \frac{\text{arc length}}{\text{radius}}$.

1. The image shows a circle with radius 1 unit.

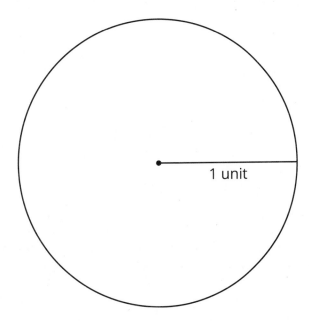

1 unit

a. Cut a piece of string that is the length of the radius of this circle.

b. Use the string to mark an arc on the circle that is the same length as the radius.

c. Draw the central angle defined by the arc.

d. Use the definition of radian to calculate the radian measure of the central angle you drew.

2. Draw a 180 degree central angle (a diameter) in the circle. Use your 1-unit piece of string to measure the approximate length of the arc defined by this angle.

3. Calculate the radian measure of the 180 degree angle. Give your answer both in terms of π and as a decimal rounded to the nearest hundredth.

4. Calculate the radian measure of a 360 degree angle.

Are you ready for more?

Research where the "360" in 360 degrees comes from. Why did people choose to define a degree as $\frac{1}{360}$ of the circumference of a circle?

Lesson 11 Summary

Degrees are one way to measure the size of an angle. **Radians** are another way to measure angles. Assume an angle's vertex is the center of a circle. The radian measure of the angle is the ratio between the length of the arc defined by the angle and the radius of the circle. We can write this as $\theta = \frac{\text{arc length}}{\text{radius}}$. This ratio is constant for a given angle, no matter the size of the circle.

Consider a 180 degree central angle in a circle with radius 3 units. The arc length defined by the angle is 3π units. The radian measure of the angle is the ratio of the arc length to the radius, which is π radians because $\frac{3\pi}{3} = \pi$.

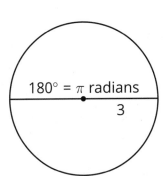

Another way to think of the radian measure of the angle is that it measures the number of radii that would make up the length of the arc defined by the angle. For example, if we draw an arc that is the same length as the radius, both the arc length and the radius are 1 unit. The radian measure of the central angle that defines this arc is the quotient of those values, or 1 radian.

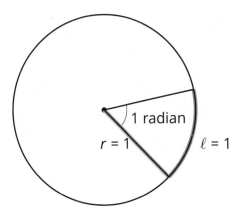

Glossary

- radian

Lesson 11 Practice Problems

1. Here is a central angle that measures 1.5 radians. Select **all** true statements.

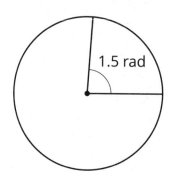

A. The radius is 1.5 times longer than the length of the arc defined by the angle.

B. The length of the arc defined by the angle is 1.5 times longer than the radius.

C. The ratio of arc length to radius is 1.5.

D. The ratio of radius to arc length is 1.5.

E. The area of the whole circle is 1.5 times the area of the slice.

F. The circumference of the whole circle is 1.5 times the length of the arc formed by the angle.

2. Match each arc length ℓ and radius r with the measure of the central angle of the arc in radians.

A. $r = 2, \ell = \frac{\pi}{2}$

B. $r = 3, \ell = 2$

C. $r = 3.5, \ell = 2.8$

D. $r = 4, \ell = 3$

E. $r = 5, \ell = \pi$

F. $r = 6, \ell = 4$

1. $\frac{\pi}{5}$ radians

2. $\frac{2}{3}$ radians

3. 0.75 radians

4. $\frac{\pi}{4}$ radians

5. 0.8 radians

3. Han thinks that since the arc length in circle A is longer, its central angle is larger. Do you agree with Han? Show or explain your reasoning.

circle A

circle B

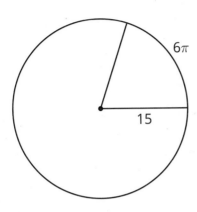

4. Circle B is a dilation of circle A.

circle A

circle B

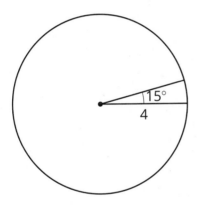

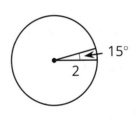

a. What is the scale factor?

b. What is the area of the 15 degree sector in circle A?

c. What is the area of the 15 degree sector in circle B?

d. What is the ratio of the areas of the sectors?

e. How does the ratio of areas of the sectors compare to the scale factor?

(From Unit 7, Lesson 10.)

5. Priya and Noah are riding different size Ferris wheels at a carnival. They started at the same time. The highlighted arcs show how far they have traveled.

Noah's Ferris wheel **Priya's Ferris wheel**

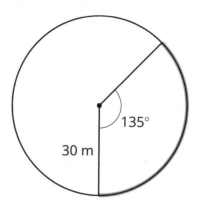

   a. How far has Noah traveled?

   b. How far has Priya traveled?

   c. If the Ferris wheels will each complete 1 revolution, who do you think will finish first?

(From Unit 7, Lesson 10.)

6. A circle has radius 8 units, and a central angle is drawn in. The length of the arc defined by the central angle is 4π units. Find the area of the sector outlined by this arc.

(From Unit 7, Lesson 9.)

7. Clare is trying to explain how to find the area of a sector of a circle. She says, "First, you find the area of the whole circle. Then, you divide by the radius." Do you agree with Clare? Explain or show your reasoning.

(From Unit 7, Lesson 8.)

8. Line BD is tangent to a circle with diameter AB. List 2 right angles.

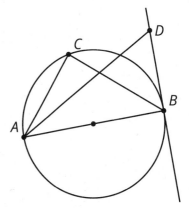

(From Unit 7, Lesson 3.)

Lesson 12: Radian Sense

- Let's get a sense for the sizes of angles measured in radians.

12.1: Which One Doesn't Belong: Angle Measures

Which one doesn't belong?

A

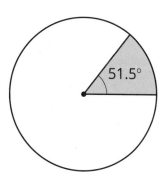

B

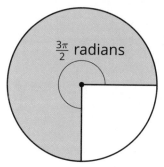

C

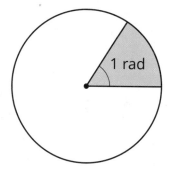

D

Geometry **iM KH**

12.2: Degrees Versus Radians

This double number line shows degree measurements on one line and radians on another.

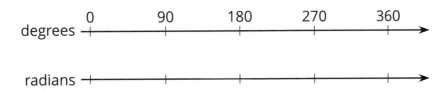

1. Fill in the radian measures on the bottom line for 0°, 90°, 180°, 270°, and 360°.

2. Express each radian measurement in degrees.
   a. $\frac{\pi}{3}$ radians

   b. $\frac{5\pi}{4}$ radians

3. Express each degree measurement in radians.
   a. 30°

   b. 120°

Are you ready for more?

Your boat is heading due south when you hear that you must head north-east to return home. You turn the boat, traveling in a counterclockwise circular path until you're facing north-east.

1. Sketch the path of the boat.

2. If the circle you traced had a radius of 40 feet, what distance did you travel?

12.3: Pie Coloring Contest

Your teacher will give you a set of cards with angle measures on them. Place the cards upside down in a pile. Choose 1 student to go first. This student should draw a card, then on either circle shade a sector of the circle whose central angle is the measure on the card that was drawn.

Take turns repeating these steps. If you are shading in a circle that already has a shaded sector, choose a spot next to the already-shaded sectors—don't leave any gaps. You might have to draw additional lines to break the sectors into smaller pieces.

Continue until an angle is drawn that won't fit in any of the sectors that are still blank.

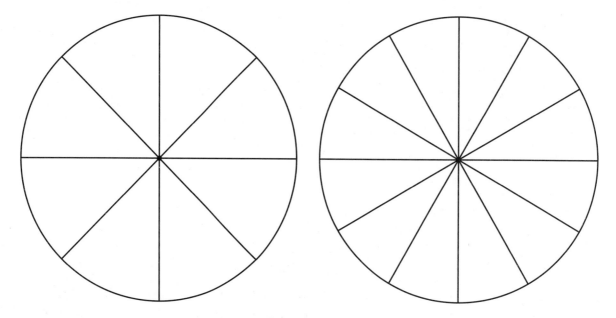

When you're finished, answer these questions about each circle:

1. What is the central angle measure for the remaining unshaded sector?

2. What is the central angle measure for the block of shaded sectors?

Geometry iM **KH**

Lesson 12 Summary

We can divide circles into congruent sectors to get a sense for the size of an angle measured in radians.

Suppose we want to draw an angle that measures $\frac{2\pi}{3}$ radians. We know that π radians is equivalent to 180 degrees. If we divide a sector with a central angle of π radians into thirds, we can shade in 2 of them to create an angle measuring $\frac{2\pi}{3}$ radians.

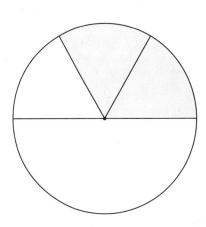

Another way to understand the size of an angle measured in radians is to create a double number line with degrees on one line and radians on the other. On the double number line in the image, the degree measurements are aligned with their equivalent radian measures. For example, π radians is equivalent to 180°.

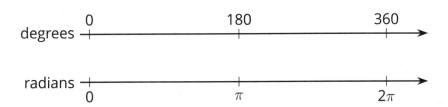

Suppose we need to know the size of an angle that measures $\frac{3\pi}{4}$ radians. The left half of the double number line represents π radians. Divide the left half of the top and bottom number lines into fourths, then count out 3 of them on the radians line to land on $\frac{3\pi}{4}$. On the top line, each interval we drew represents 45 degrees because $180 \div 4 = 45$. If we count 3 of those intervals, we find that $\frac{3\pi}{4}$ radians is equivalent to 135 degrees because $45 \cdot 3 = 135$.

Lesson 12 Practice Problems

1. Match each diagram showing a sector with the measure of its central angle in radians.

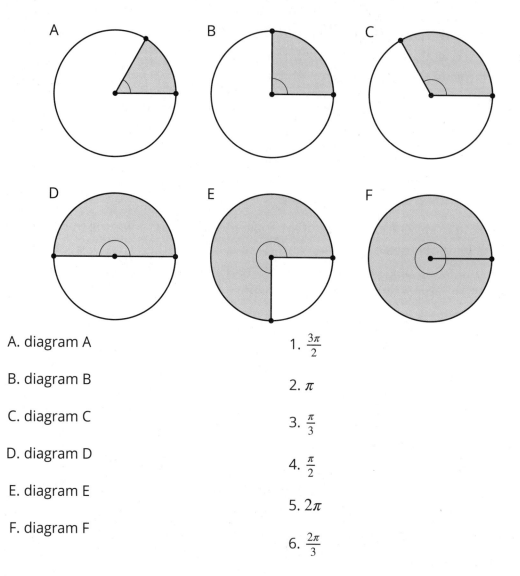

A. diagram A

B. diagram B

C. diagram C

D. diagram D

E. diagram E

F. diagram F

1. $\frac{3\pi}{2}$

2. π

3. $\frac{\pi}{3}$

4. $\frac{\pi}{2}$

5. 2π

6. $\frac{2\pi}{3}$

2. In the circle, sketch a central angle that measures $\frac{2\pi}{3}$ radians.

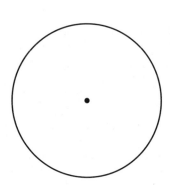

Geometry iM KH

3. Angle AOC has a measure of $\frac{5\pi}{6}$ radians. The length of arc AB is 2π units and the radius is 12 units. What is the area of sector BOC?

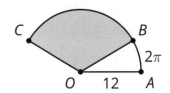

4. Calculate the radian measure of a 30 degree angle. Use any method you like, including sketching in the circle diagram provided. Explain or show your reasoning.

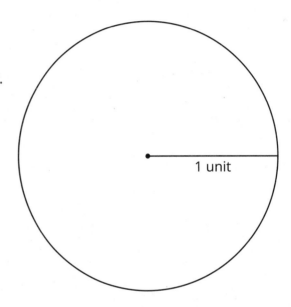

1 unit

(From Unit 7, Lesson 11.)

5. Lin thinks that the central angle in circle A is congruent to the central angle in circle B. Do you agree with Lin? Show or explain your reasoning.

circle A

circle B

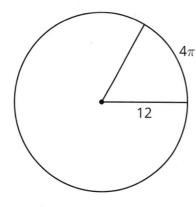

(From Unit 7, Lesson 11.)

6. **circle A**

circle B

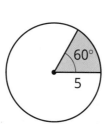

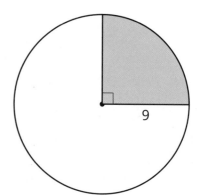

Select **all** true statements.

A. The sector in circle B has a larger area than the sector in circle A.

B. Not taking into account the sectors, circle A and circle B are similar.

C. The fraction of the circumference taken up by the arc outlining circle A's sector is smaller than the fraction of the circumference taken up by the arc in circle B.

D. The ratio of the area of circle A's sector to its total area is $\frac{1}{6}$.

E. The ratio of circle A's area to circle B's area is $\frac{5}{9}$.

(From Unit 7, Lesson 10.)

Geometry **iM KH**

7. Match each arc length and radius with the measure of the central angle that defines the arc.

    A. arc length 5π cm, radius 5 cm   1. angle: 30 degrees

    B. arc length 4π cm, radius 10 cm   2. angle: 72 degrees

    C. arc length 9π cm, radius 12 cm   3. angle: 135 degrees

    D. arc length 3π cm, radius 18 cm   4. angle: 180 degrees

(From Unit 7, Lesson 9.)

8. Quadrilateral $ABCD$ is shown with the given angle measures. Select **all** true statements.

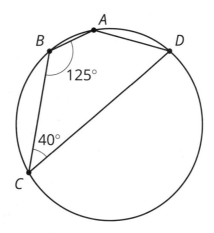

    A. Angle A measures 140 degrees.

    B. The measures of angle A and angle D must add to 180 degrees.

    C. Angle A measures 55 degrees.

    D. Angle D measures 55 degrees.

    E. Angle D measures 40 degrees.

(From Unit 7, Lesson 4.)

Lesson 13: Using Radians

- Let's see how radians can help us calculate sector areas and arc lengths.

13.1: What Fraction?

A circle with radius 24 inches has a sector with central angle $\frac{\pi}{3}$ radians.

1. What fraction of the whole circle is represented by this sector?

2. Find the area of the sector.

13.2: A Sector Area Shortcut

Lin and Elena are trying to find the area of the shaded sector in the image. Lin says, "We've found sector areas when the central angle is given in degrees, but here it's in radians. Should I start by finding the area of the full circle?"

Elena says, "I saw someone using the formula $\frac{1}{2}r^2\theta$ where θ is the measure of the angle in radians, and r is the radius. But I don't know where that came from."

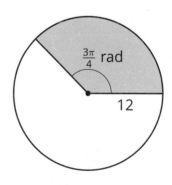

1. Compare and contrast finding sector areas for central angles measured in degrees and those measured in radians.

Geometry iM KH

2. Explain why the formula that Elena saw works.

3. Find the area of the sector.

13.3: An Arc Length Shortcut

The city of Riverside has 2 straight highways extending out from its town hall (located at T in the image). Several roads shaped like circular arcs connect the two highways. Exits from 1 of the highways are shown at points A, B, C, and D.

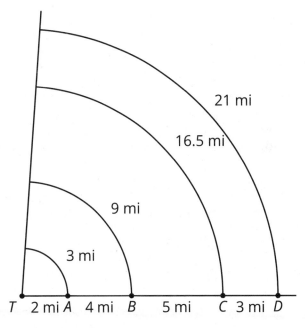

1. Create a table that shows the arc length, ℓ, of the connector roads as a function of the radius, r, of the highway.

2. Plot the points from your table on the coordinate grid and connect them.

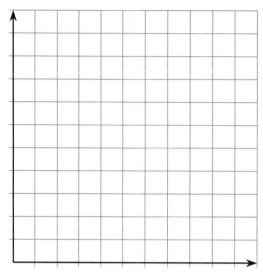

3. The points should form a line. Write an equation for this line, using the variables ℓ and r.

4. What does the slope of the line mean in context of the highways and connector roads?

5. The city wants to build a new arc-shaped connector road starting at point E which will be an additional 6 miles past exit D. How long will this road be?

Are you ready for more?

Suppose a Ferris wheel with a 50 foot radius takes 2 minutes to complete 1 rotation.

1. After 20 seconds, through how many radians would a rider on the Ferris wheel have traveled?

2. How long would it take to travel through 3 radians?

3. What is the rotational speed of the rider on the ferris wheel in radians per second?

4. A decorative light is attached to the Ferris wheel 25 feet from the center of the wheel. What is the rotational speed of the light in radians per second?

Lesson 13 Summary

Suppose we want to find the area of a sector of a circle whose central angle is θ radians and whose radius is r units. First we find the area of the whole circle, or πr^2 square units. Then we find the fraction of the circle represented by the sector. The complete circle measures 2π radians. So the fraction is $\frac{\theta}{2\pi}$. Multiply the fraction by the area to get $\frac{\theta}{2\pi} \cdot \pi r^2$. This can be rewritten as $\frac{1}{2} r^2 \theta$.

For example, let the radius be 25 units and the radian measure of the sector's central angle be $\frac{3\pi}{5}$ radians. Substitute these values into the formula we just created to get $\frac{1}{2}(25)^2 \cdot \frac{3\pi}{5}$. This can be rewritten as $\frac{375\pi}{2}$, which is about 589 square units. Using the formula was a bit quicker than going through the process of finding the specific fraction of the circle represented by this sector and multiplying by the circle's area.

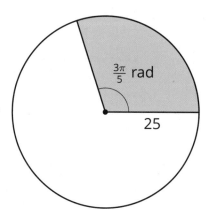

Additionally, we can write a formula for arc length based on the definition of radian measure as $\theta = \frac{\ell}{r}$ where θ is the central angle measure in radians, ℓ is the arc length, and r is the radius. Rewrite the definition to solve for arc length. We get $\ell = r\theta$.

Geometry iM KH

Lesson 13 Practice Problems

1. a. Find the arc length of an arc with a central angle of $\frac{2\pi}{3}$ radians and a radius of 6 units.

   b. Find the arc length of an arc with a central angle of $\frac{5\pi}{6}$ radians and a circumference of 12 units.

   c. Find the measure (in radians) of a central angle of an arc with arc length 4 units and radius 3 units.

2. A circle has radius 10 units. For each angle measure, find the area of a sector of this circle with that central angle.

   a. $\frac{\pi}{8}$ radians

   b. $\frac{3\pi}{4}$ radians

   c. 1 radian

   d. 2 radians

3. Each circle has a shaded sector with a central angle measured in radians. What fraction of the circle is each sector?

circle A   **circle B**   **circle C**

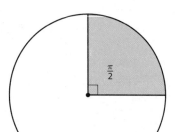 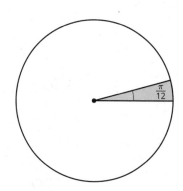 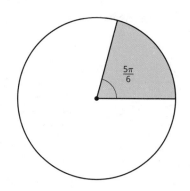

4. Find the radian measure of each angle.

   a. 30 degrees

   b. 45 degrees

   c. 50 degrees

   (From Unit 7, Lesson 12.)

5. Find the degree measure of each angle.

   a. $\frac{\pi}{3}$ radians

   b. $\frac{\pi}{2}$ radians

   c. $\frac{3\pi}{4}$ radians

   d. 3 radians

   (From Unit 7, Lesson 12.)

6. Calculate the radian measure of a 225 degree angle. Use any method you like, including sketching in the circle diagram provided. Explain or show your reasoning.

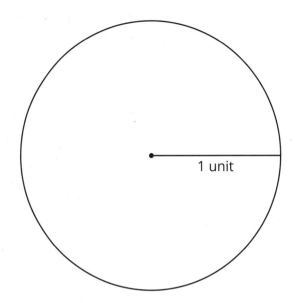

1 unit

(From Unit 7, Lesson 11.)

7. **Andre's circle**   **Diego's circle**

270°
10 cm

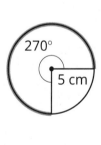

270°
5 cm

Andre and Diego are each saving money. They each hope to save 500 dollars. They are tracking their progress on the circles in the image.

Diego thinks that Andre has saved more money than Diego has saved. Andre thinks they have saved the same amount. Do you agree with either of them? Explain or show your reasoning.

(From Unit 7, Lesson 10.)

8. Clare missed class and Jada is teaching her how to construct the circumscribed circle of a triangle. Here are the instructions Jada wrote.

"Construct all 3 perpendicular bisectors of the triangle's sides. The point where the perpendicular bisectors intersect is called the circumcenter. Construct a circle centered at the circumcenter with radius set to the distance between the circumcenter and a vertex. If the triangle has a circumscribed circle, the circle you construct will go through all 3 vertices."

Do you agree with Jada's instructions? Explain your reasoning.

(From Unit 7, Lesson 5.)

Lesson 14: Putting It All Together

- Let's use geometry to solve problems.

14.1: Equal Slices

At a pizza restaurant, a personal pizza has a radius of 10 centimeters and costs $5. Another restaurant takes a pizza with radius 30 centimeters, cuts it into 8 slices of equal area, and charges $5 per slice. Which is a better deal? Explain your reasoning.

14.2: Pizza Palooza

Elena was researching offers for the upcoming Pizza Palooza festival. She wants to get a good deal on a single slice of pizza.

Your teacher will give you cards that show the deals offered by 4 vendors. Which vendor should Elena choose? Explain or show your reasoning.

14.3: A Fair Split

Jada and Andre want to share a big slice of pizza so that each of them gets the same amount, but Andre doesn't like the crust. The pizza slice is a sector of a circle with a radius of 20 cm and a central angle that measures $\frac{\pi}{3}$ radians.

How can Andre and Jada divide the slice of pizza into 2 equal pieces so that Andre doesn't have to eat any crust?

14.4: Let Your Light Shine

Noah is taking photos of a sculpture he made in art class. He will submit the photos to a contest. The sculpture is in front of a backdrop, which is represented from an overhead view in the image by segment AB. Noah positioned a light at point C so that the edges of the light beam meet up exactly with the backdrop at segment AB.

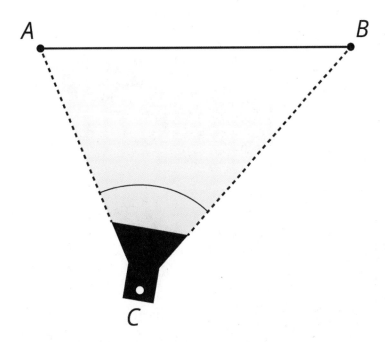

Noah wants to try different positions for the light to highlight different aspects of the sculpture, but he still wants the edges of the beam to exactly meet the endpoints of the backdrop. Find at least 3 other places Noah can place the light. Explain or show your reasoning.

Lesson 14 Summary

We can use sector areas to compare the value of product offers. Suppose the manager of a store wants to buy several dozen mirrors shaped like sectors of a circle to decorate the store. The manager is choosing between these 2 brands of mirrors at a tradeshow. Brand A's mirror has radius 14 inches and costs $35 for each sector. Brand B's mirror has radius 15 inches and costs $42. Which is the better deal in terms of cost per square inch of mirror?

brand A   **brand B**

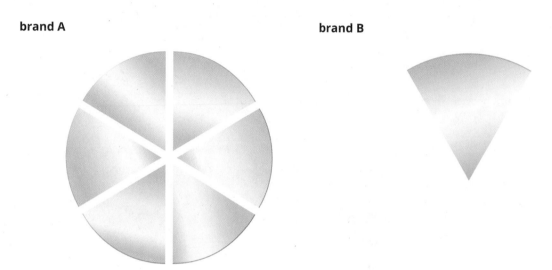

Brand A's mirror is made from a circle cut into 6 congruent slices. Using the expression πr^2 with radius 14 inches, we find that the area of the full circle is 196π or about 616 square inches. Divide that by 6 to find that each sector-shaped mirror has an area of about 103 square inches. At $35 per sector, this mirror costs about $0.34 per square inch.

For brand B, we don't know how many slices the mirror was cut into. However, we can estimate the measure of the central angle using arc length and radius. Suppose the manager uses a flexible measuring tape to find that the length of the arc around the outside of the sector is 19 inches. The ratio of the arc length to the radius gives the measure of the central angle in radians, $\frac{19}{15}$. This is about 1.27 radians, but to avoid rounding errors, let's use the exact value, $\frac{19}{15}$, in our calculations.

Next, we can find the area of the sector with the formula $\frac{1}{2}r^2\theta$ where r is the radius and θ is the radian measure of the central angle. Substitute in our values to get $\frac{1}{2}(15)^2 \cdot \frac{19}{15}$, or 142.5 square centimeters. At $42 per sector, this mirror costs about $0.29 per square inch. Brand B's mirror is a better deal.

Lesson 14 Practice Problems

1. Jada is finding the area of a sector with an angle $\frac{\pi}{4}$ radians and radius 8 units. She found the area of the whole circle, then found the fraction represented by the sector by dividing $\frac{\pi}{4}$ by 360. She multiplied this fraction by the total circle area.

   a. Do you agree with Jada's strategy? Explain your reasoning.

   b. Find the area of the sector.

   (From Unit 7, Lesson 13.)

2. Which of these pizza slices gives the best value (the most pizza per dollar spent)?

   A. a slice with a radius of 12 inches, central angle of 30°, and a cost of $3 per slice

   B. a slice with a radius of 8 inches, central angle of 45°, and a cost of $2 per slice

   C. a slice with a radius of 6 inches, central angle of $\frac{\pi}{3}$ radians, and a cost of $2 per slice

   D. a slice with a radius of 6 inches, central angle of $\frac{\pi}{4}$ radians, and a cost of $1 per slice

   (From Unit 7, Lesson 13.)

3. The circle in the image has been divided into congruent sectors. What is the measure of the central angle of the shaded region in radians?

   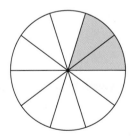

   (From Unit 7, Lesson 12.)

4. In the circle, sketch a central angle that measures $\frac{5\pi}{3}$ radians.

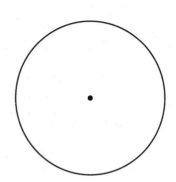

(From Unit 7, Lesson 12.)

5. The image shows a circle with radius 5 units.

   a. Draw a 180 degree central angle (a diameter) in the circle. What is the length of the arc defined by this angle?

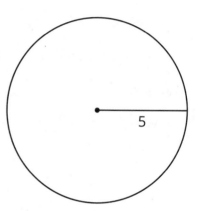

   b. Use the arc length and the radius to calculate the radian measure of 180 degrees.

   c. Calculate the radian measure of a 360 degree angle. Explain or show your reasoning.

(From Unit 7, Lesson 11.)

6. Complete the table. Each row represents a circle with a defined sector.

sector area	radius	central angle
5π cm^2	5 cm	
12π cm^2		270 degrees
	12 cm	15 degrees

(From Unit 7, Lesson 9.)

7. Several circles with central angles are described. Select **all** the circles for which the central angle defines arcs that have length 6π units.

    A. radius 6 units, central angle 180 degrees

    B. radius 18 units, central angle 60 degrees

    C. radius 12 units, central angle 90 degrees

    D. radius 3 units, central angle 120 degrees

    E. radius 4 units, central angle 270 degrees

(From Unit 7, Lesson 8.)

8. Triangle ABC is shown with its incenter at D. The inscribed circle's radius measures 2 units. The length of AB is 9 units. The length of BC is 10 units. The length of AC is 17 units.

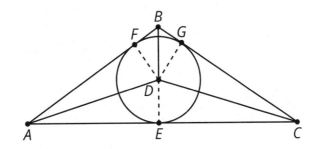

a. What is the area of triangle ABD?

b. What is the area of triangle BCD?

(From Unit 7, Lesson 7.)

9. Noah makes 3 statements about the incenter of a triangle.

a. To find the incenter of a triangle, you must construct all 3 angle bisectors.

b. The incenter is always equidistant from the vertices of the triangle.

c. The incenter is always equidistant from each side of the triangle.

For each statement, decide whether you agree with Noah. Explain your reasoning.

(From Unit 7, Lesson 6.)

10. Elena is writing notes about central angles in circles. Help her finish her notes by answering the questions.

a. Where is the vertex of a central angle located in relation to the circle?

b. What line segments related to circles are contained in the rays that form a central angle?

c. How does the measure of a central angle relate to the measure of the arc it intersects?

(From Unit 7, Lesson 1.)

Learning Targets

Lesson 1: Lines, Angles, and Curves

- I know what chords, arcs, and central angles are.

Lesson 2: Inscribed Angles

- I can use the relationship between central and inscribed angles to calculate angle measures and prove geometric theorems.

- I know that an inscribed angle is half the measure of the central angle that defines the same arc.

Lesson 3: Tangent Lines

- I can use the relationship between tangent lines and radii to calculate angle measures and prove geometric theorems.

- I know that a line tangent to a circle is perpendicular to the radius drawn to the point of tangency.

Lesson 4: Quadrilaterals in Circles

- I can prove a theorem about opposite angles in quadrilaterals inscribed in circles.

Lesson 5: Triangles in Circles

- I can construct the circumscribed circle of a triangle.

- I can explain why the perpendicular bisectors of a triangle's sides meet at a single point.

Lesson 6: A Special Point

- I can explain why the angle bisectors of a triangle meet at a single point.

- I know any point on an angle bisector is equidistant from the rays that form the angle.

Lesson 7: Circles in Triangles

- I can construct the inscribed circle of a triangle.

Lesson 8: Arcs and Sectors

- I can calculate lengths of arcs and areas of sectors in circles.

Lesson 9: Part to Whole

- I can gather information about a sector to draw conclusions about the entire circle.

Lesson 10: Angles, Arcs, and Radii

- I know that when a circle is dilated, some ratios, like the ratio of the circumference to the diameter, stay constant.

Lesson 11: A New Way to Measure Angles

- I know that the radian measure of an angle whose vertex is the center of a circle is the ratio of the length of the arc defined by the angle to the circle's radius.

Lesson 12: Radian Sense

- I understand the relative sizes of angles measured in radians.

Lesson 13: Using Radians

- I can calculate the area of a sector whose central angle measure is given in radians.

- I know that the radian measure of an angle can be thought of as the slope of the line $\ell = \theta \cdot r$.

Lesson 14: Putting It All Together

- I can use properties of circles to solve geometric problems.

GEOMETRY

STUDENT WORKBOOK

Book 3

Lesson 1: Up to Chance

- Let's explore chance.

1.1: Which One Doesn't Belong: Spinners

Which one doesn't belong?

A

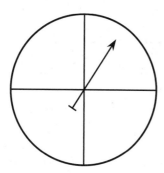

B

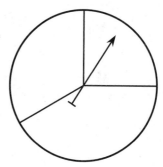

C

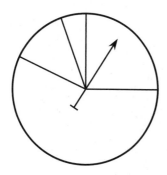

D

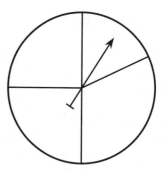

1.2: You're Saying There's a Chance?

In Elena's Spanish class, they have a quiz every two weeks.

- For the first quiz of the year, Elena takes time to study and understands the material very well. The quiz involves 20 multiple choice questions with possible answers A, B, C, or D. Elena tries her best to answer the questions correctly.

- For the second quiz of the year, Elena has been absent a lot and does not understand the material at all. The quiz involves 20 multiple choice questions with possible answers A, B, C, or D. Elena fills in the answer sheet without even looking at the questions.

- For the third quiz of the year, Elena is still lost in the class and has not come in for any help. The quiz involves 20 true or false questions. Again, Elena fills in the answer sheet without even looking at the questions.

1. Based on the description, rank the quizzes in order from worst expected grade to best.

2. For each of the 3 quizzes, explain why you think chance played a large or small role in determining Elena's score.

3. For the second and third quizzes, Elena did not look at the questions. Explain why you think she might do better on one than the other.

4. What percentage of the questions do you think Elena will get right on each quiz? Explain your reasoning.

5. For the second quiz, the teacher made a mistake and each of the questions had two correct answers. The teacher accepted either of the correct answers for full credit. What percentage of the questions do you think Elena will get right on the second quiz with the new scoring? Explain your reasoning.

1.3: A Fair Game

Han, Clare, Mai, and Kiran are inventing a game for the county fair. Players will spin a spinner and if it points to the section labeled B, then the player will win a prize.

Han says, "I think this spinner is a good one. What do you think?"

Clare says, "I like the spinner, but I think people should be able to spin again if they don't win the first time."

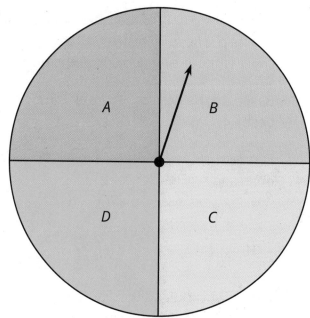

Mai says, "What if we just make 3 sections like this?"

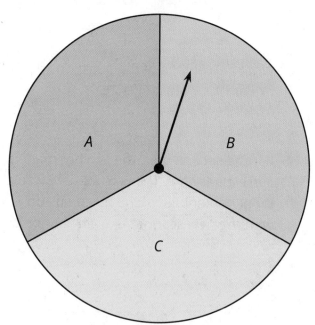

Kiran says, "I think it might make more sense if we just do two sections like this."

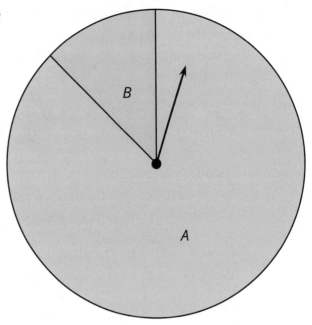

1. Put the proposals in order of the **probability** that a player will win using that method from least to greatest. Explain your reasoning. Share your explanation with a partner.

2. Each student writes a computer program to play the game using the method they suggested. The computer runs the program for a short time and reports the number of wins and losses. Use the results to estimate the probability of winning using each method.

   ○ Han's method: 2,513 wins; 7,516 losses.

   ○ Clare's method: 876 wins; 1,127 losses.

   ○ Mai's method: 2,026 wins; 3,984 losses.

   ○ Kiran's method: 322 wins; 3,621 losses.

3. By talking to their friends, they figure out that a good probability for winning is about $\frac{1}{5}$ since it will let enough people win to draw in customers, but not cost them too much for prizes. Which method fits this best?

4. Before they settled on a spinner game, they considered other things at their booth. Which of these suggestions would be considered chance experiments?

- A watermelon-eating contest. The fastest to eat a wedge of watermelon wins the prize.

- Two cubes have one face labeled "Win!" If both cubes land with the "Win!" side facing up, the player wins a prize.

- A ball is placed under one of five cups. The cups are shuffled around under a cover so the player cannot see how they are moved. The player chooses one of the cups and wins a prize if it has the ball under it.

- Players push a button that starts lighting up different regions on a board. The game is rigged so that every fifth person wins.

Are you ready for more?

1. Draw a spinner with 3 or more sections that are not all the same size.

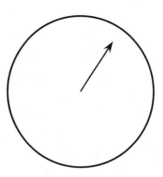

2. Your spinner is spun 1,000 times. Estimate the number of times you would expect the spinner to land on each section. Explain your reasoning.

3. A different spinner with only two sections is spun 1,000 times. It landed on one section 136 times and the other section 864 times. Draw a spinner that is likely to produce similar results if spun 1,000 times. Explain your reasoning.

Geometry iM KH

Lesson 1 Summary

Few things are certain in life, but we can look more closely at uncertain processes, called chance experiments, to get a better idea of the likelihood of a particular thing happening. Lots of times, it is possible to recognize several different results that may happen. These results are called outcomes. The collection of all possible outcomes is called the sample space. An event is a group of outcomes from the sample space.

For example, flipping a coin is a chance experiment that has possible outcomes of landing with heads facing up or tails facing up. Sometimes, one outcome is more likely than another. For example, when walking outside in a thunderstorm, it is much more likely you will get hit by a raindrop than a lightning bolt.

To put a number to this likelihood is to find or estimate its **probability**. The probability of a chance event is a number between 0 and 1 that expresses the likelihood of the event occurring. It is estimated that the probability of getting hit by lightning in the United States in one year is about $\frac{1}{700,000}$, which means that, each year in the United States, a person has a 0.00014% ($1 \div 700,000 \approx 0.0000014$) chance of getting hit by lightning.

Glossary

- chance experiment
- event
- outcome
- probability
- sample space

Lesson 1 Practice Problems

1. What is the probability of the spinner landing on the section labeled G?

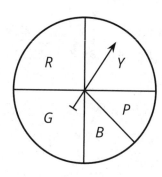

   A. $\frac{1}{2}$

   B. $\frac{1}{4}$

   C. $\frac{1}{5}$

   D. $\frac{1}{8}$

2. This spinner is spun 1,000 times. Which of these is the best estimate for the number of times it would be expected to land on the section labeled B?

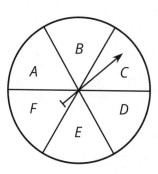

   A. 16

   B. 60

   C. 160

   D. 600

Geometry iM KH

3. On an assignment, there are two true or false questions. You have no idea what the correct answer is to either one so you guess.

    a. What is the probability that you get both of them right by guessing? Explain your answer.

    b. What is the probability that you get exactly one of them right by guessing? Explain your answer.

4.   a. Find the length of an arc with central angle $\frac{2\pi}{3}$ radians and a radius of 7 units.

    b. Find the length of an arc with central angle $\frac{\pi}{4}$ radians and a circumference of 10π units.

    c. Find the measure (in radians) of a central angle of an arc with arc length 12 units and radius 3 units.

(From Unit 7, Lesson 13.)

5. In the circle, sketch a central angle that measures $\frac{\pi}{2}$ radians.

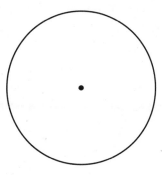

(From Unit 7, Lesson 12.)

6. The circle in the image has been divided into congruent sectors. What is the measure of the central angle of the shaded region in radians?

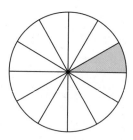

A. $\frac{1}{12}$ radians

B. $\frac{\pi}{12}$ radians

C. $\frac{1}{6}$ radians

D. $\frac{\pi}{6}$ radians

(From Unit 7, Lesson 12.)

7. Select **all** true statements.

A. The incenter of a triangle is the intersection of the angle bisectors.

B. The incenter is the same distance from all the vertices of the triangle.

C. The incenter is the same distance from all sides of the triangle.

D. In order to construct the incenter, all 3 angle bisectors must be constructed.

E. The incenter is the intersection of the perpendicular bisectors of each side.

(From Unit 7, Lesson 6.)

Geometry iM KH

Lesson 2: Playing with Probability

- Let's explore probability

2.1: Taking Names

Your teacher will give your group a bag containing slips of paper with names on them. It is important not to open the bag to read the slips at any time. It is important to record your group's data in writing.

Every time a student in the class is notably helpful, a teacher puts their name on a slip of paper and puts it into a bag. If the same student is helpful more than once, their name can be entered multiple times. At the end of the month, the teacher draws several names for prizes. Follow these steps to collect data about the names in the bag:

1. Shake the bag, then draw out only 1 slip of paper.

2. Read the name you drew out loud so that everyone in the group can record the name.

3. Return the slip of paper to the bag and pass the bag to the next person in the group.

4. Repeat these steps until each person in the group has had a chance to draw at least 3 names.

2.2: Who Was Helpful?

Use the data your group collected in the warm-up to answer the questions.

1. Based on the data you collected, estimate the probability of drawing each of these names from your bag. Explain or show your reasoning.

   a. Clare

   b. Lin

   c. Priya

   d. Elena

   e. Jada

   f. Han

   g. Andre

   h. Diego

   i. Noah

2. There are 15 slips of paper in the bag. What names do you think are written on the slips? Explain your reasoning.

3. If you are allowed to keep going around the group, drawing names and replacing them until you had 100 names drawn, how do you think that affects your understanding of what is in the bag?

4. The next month, the bag contains 15 slips as well. Lin's name is included 5 times, Clare's name 4 times, Han's name 3 times, Diego's name 2 times, and Jada's name 1 time. The teacher draws names one at a time, replacing them each time. What might the teacher's list of names drawn look like if she draws 10 times? Is this the only list of names drawn that is possible? Explain your reasoning.

2.3: Probability Words

Take turns with your partner coming up with words that have the probabilities given when selecting a letter at random from the word. Each person should try to come up with one word for each situation.

1. $P(\text{vowel}) = \frac{1}{3}$. $P(\text{consonant}) = \frac{2}{3}$.

2. $P(\text{vowel}) = \frac{2}{3}$. $P(\text{consonant}) = \frac{1}{3}$.

3. $P(\text{vowel}) = 0.5$. $P(\text{T}) = \frac{1}{4}$.

4. $P(\text{S}) = 0.5$. $P(\text{vowel}) = 0.25$.

5. Think of a word and give your partner at least 2 clues about the word using probability of certain letters or types of letter.

Are you ready for more?

Each of the whole numbers from 1 to 25 is written on a slip of paper and placed in a bag.

1. Calculate each probability.
    a. $P(\text{prime})$

    b. $P(\text{divisible by 3 but not 2})$

    c. $P(\text{multiple of 5})$

    d. $P(\text{greater than 20})$

    e. $P(\text{multiple of 12 and less than 20})$

2. Use this situation to create two of your own probability questions that give a probability of $\frac{1}{25}$ as the answer.

3. Use this situation to create two of your own probability questions that give a probability of $\frac{3}{25}$ as the answer.

Lesson 2 Summary

Some probabilities are estimated by doing an experiment, or sometimes simulating the experiment many times and collecting data about how often outcomes come up. For example, a radio show holds a contest in which callers are entered for a chance to win a ticket to a concert in town. The probability of each caller winning is estimated by considering previous similar contests and comparing the number of callers to the number of ticket winners. If a previous contest had 327 callers and 5 ticket winners, then the probability of winning a ticket can be written:

$$P(\text{winning a ticket}) = \frac{5}{327} \text{ or } P(\text{winning a ticket}) \approx 0.015$$

Which means that each caller has about a 1.5% chance of winning a ticket to the concert.

Other probabilities can be determined by recognizing the expected relative likelihood of outcomes among all possible outcomes. For example, we know that the probability of rolling a 2 on a standard number cube is $\frac{1}{6}$ since there are 6 equally likely outcomes in the sample space for each roll and the event of rolling a 2 is one of those outcomes. This can be written as $P(\text{rolling a 2}) = \frac{1}{6}$.

Lesson 2 Practice Problems

1. Six papers are placed in a bag with names written on them. The names are: Lin, Mai, Mai, Noah, Priya, and Priya. If one name is chosen at random, what is the probability that it is Priya?

    A. $\frac{1}{4}$

    B. $\frac{1}{6}$

    C. $\frac{2}{4}$

    D. $\frac{2}{6}$

2. Select **all** of the words for which the probability of selecting the letter E at random is $\frac{1}{3}$.

    A. THE

    B. BEST

    C. SNEEZE

    D. FREES

    E. SPEECH

3. Design a situation where the probability of one event is $\frac{1}{5}$ and another event is $\frac{1}{10}$. Explain your reasoning.

4. What is the probability of the spinner landing on the section labeled B?

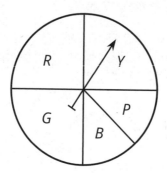

A. $\frac{1}{8}$

B. $\frac{1}{5}$

C. $\frac{1}{4}$

D. $\frac{1}{2}$

(From Unit 8, Lesson 1.)

5. This spinner is spun 300 times. Estimate the number of times it would be expected to land on the section labeled B.

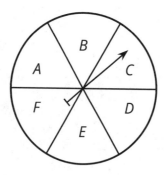

(From Unit 8, Lesson 1.)

6. A circle has radius 5 units. For each angle measure, find the area of a sector of this circle with that central angle.

   a. π radians

   b. 3 radians

(From Unit 7, Lesson 13.)

7. Select **all** formulas that could be used to find the area of this sector. The angle θ is measured in radians.

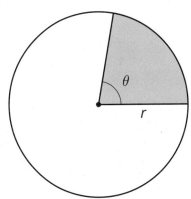

   A. $\frac{1}{2}r^2\theta$

   B. $\frac{\theta}{2\pi} \cdot \pi r^2$

   C. $\frac{\theta}{360} \cdot \pi r^2$

   D. $\frac{\pi^2}{r} \cdot \theta$

   E. $\frac{\theta}{2\pi} \cdot 2\pi r$

(From Unit 7, Lesson 13.)

8. Triangle ABC is shown with an inscribed circle of radius 4 units centered at point D. The inscribed circle is tangent to side AB at point G. The length of AG is 6 units and the length of BG is 8 units. What is the measure of angle B?

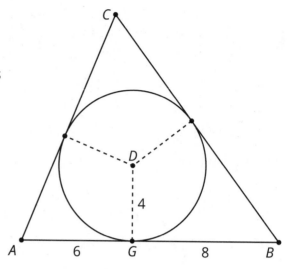

A. 60 degrees

B. 30 degrees

C. $2\arctan\left(\frac{1}{2}\right)$

D. $\arctan\left(\frac{1}{2}\right)$

(From Unit 7, Lesson 7.)

9. Select **all** the true statements.

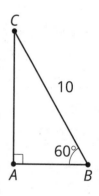

A. Angle C is 30 degrees.

B. Side AC is 5 units.

C. Side AB is 5 units.

D. Side AC is $5\sqrt{2}$ units.

E. Side AC is $10\sqrt{3}$ units.

(From Unit 4, Lesson 3.)

Geometry iM KH

Lesson 3: Sample Spaces

- Let's look closer at sample spaces.

3.1: Rolling Cubes

When rolling two standard number cubes, one of the possible outcomes is 1 and 1.

1. What are the other possible outcomes?

2. How many outcomes are in the sample space?

3.2: Spinner Sample Space

Each of the spinners is spun once.

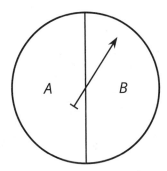 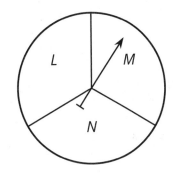 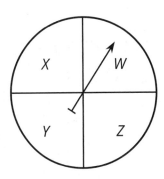

- Diego makes a list of the possible outcomes: ALW, ALX, ALY, ALZ, AMW, AMX, AMY, AMZ, ANW, ANX, ANY, ANZ, BLW, BLX, BLY, BLZ, BMW, BMX, BMY, BMZ, BNW, BNX, BNY, BNZ

- Tyler makes a table for the first two spinners.

	L	M	N
A	AL	AM	AN
B	BL	BM	BN

Then he uses the outcomes from the table to include the third spinner.

	W	X	Y	Z
AL	ALW	ALX	ALY	ALZ
AM	AMW	AMX	AMY	AMZ
AN	ANW	ANX	ANY	ANZ
BL	BLW	BLX	BLY	BLZ
BM	BMW	BMX	BMY	BMX
BN	BNW	BNX	BNY	BNZ

- Lin creates a tree to keep track of the outcomes.

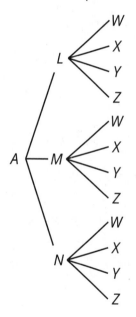
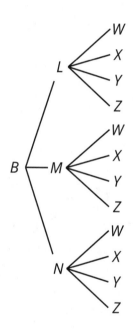

1. How many outcomes are in the sample space for this experiment?

2. One of the outcomes from Diego's list is BLX. Where does this show up in Tyler's method? Where is it in Lin's method?

3. When spinning all three spinners, what is the probability that:
    a. they point to the letters ANY? Explain your reasoning.

    b. they point to the letters AMW, ANZ, or BNW? Explain your reasoning.

4. If a fourth spinner that has 2 equal sections labeled S and T is added, how would each of the methods need to adjust?

3.3: Sample Space Practice

List all the possible outcomes for each experiment.

1. A standard number cube is rolled, then a coin is flipped.

2. Four coins are flipped.

3. The two spinners are spun.

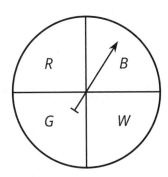 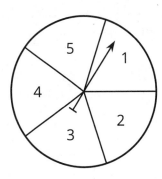

4. A class block is chosen from 1, 2, 3, 4, or 5, then a subject is chosen from English or math.

Are you ready for more?

Elena is answering a matching practice problem where she has to match each of 4 items in a left column (A, B, C, D) to 4 items on the right (1, 2, 3, 4) so that each item is used exactly once. For example one way to answer this problem is A4, B2, C1, D3.

1. What are all the possible ways she could answer this problem?

2. The actual solution is A1, B2, C3, D4. If Elena was equally likely to guess any answer, use the sample space to find:
   a. The probability of getting 0 items matched correctly.

   b. The probability of getting 1 item matched correctly.

   c. The probability of getting 2 items matched correctly.

   d. The probability of getting 3 items matched correctly.

   e. The probability of getting 2 items matched correctly.

Lesson 3 Summary

Probability represents the proportion of the time an event will occur when repeating an experiment many, many times. For complex experiments, the sample space can get very large very quickly, so it is helpful to have some methods for keeping track of the outcomes in the sample space.

In some cases, it makes sense to list all the outcomes in the sample space. For example, when flipping 3 coins, the 8 outcomes in the sample space are:

HHH, HHT, HTH, THH, HTT, THT, TTH, TTT

where H represents heads and T represents tails.

With more outcomes possible, it can be difficult to make sure all the outcomes are represented and none are repeated, so other methods may be helpful.

Another option is to use tables. When a complex experiment is broken down into parts, tables can be used to find the outcomes of two parts at a time. For example, when flipping 3 coins, we determine the outcomes for flipping just 2 coins.

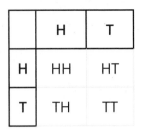

	H	T
H	HH	HT
T	TH	TT

The possible outcomes are represented by the 4 options in the middle of the table: HH, HT, TH, and TT. These outcomes can then be combined with the third coin flip in another table.

	H	T
HH	HHH	HHT
HT	HTH	HTT
TH	THH	THT
TT	TTH	TTT

Again, we see that the outcomes are HHH, HHT, HTH, HTT, THH, THT, TTH, and TTT.

Another way to keep track of the outcomes is to draw a tree structure. Each column represents another part of an experiment, with branches connecting each possible result from one part of the experiment to the possible results for the next part. By following the branches from left to right, each path represents an outcome for the sample space. The tree for flipping 3 coins would look like this:

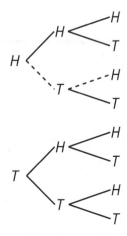

The path shown with the dashed line represents the HTH outcome. By following the other paths, the other 7 outcomes can be seen.

Lesson 3 Practice Problems

1. List all the possible outcomes for spinning the spinner and flipping a fair coin.

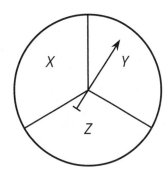

2. A student picks a random letter from the word "cat" and a random letter from the word "meow."

   a. How many outcomes are in the sample space?

   b. What is the probability that a "c" is chosen?

   c. What is the probability that a "w" is chosen?

   d. What is the probability that a "c" and a "w" are chosen?

3. Tyler decides which type of pizza to order. The choices for crust are thin crust or regular crust. The choices for one topping are pepperoni, mushrooms, olives, sausage, or green peppers. Tyler has trouble deciding because there are so many possibilities. He selects the type of crust and one topping at random. How many outcomes are in the sample space?

   A. 2

   B. 5

   C. 7

   D. 10

4. A spinner is divided into 5 equal sections. 2 of them are red, 1 of them is orange, 1 of them is yellow, and 1 of them is green.

    a. What is the probability that it lands on red?

    b. What is the probability that it lands on orange or yellow?

    c. What is the probability that it lands on blue?

(From Unit 8, Lesson 2.)

5. Select **all** of the situations that have a 25% chance of occurring.

    A. Rolling a standard number cube and getting a 4.

    B. Flipping two fair coins and getting heads on the first flip and tails on the second flip.

    C. Picking a letter at random from the word KALAMATA and getting an A.

    D. Picking a letter at random from the word CALAMITY and getting an A.

    E. Getting the correct answer when guessing randomly on a multiple choice question that has 4 choices.

(From Unit 8, Lesson 1.)

6. A circle has radius 12 inches, and a central angle is drawn in. The length of the arc defined by the central angle is 20π inches. Find the area of the sector outlined by this arc.

(From Unit 7, Lesson 9.)

7. Here is a straightedge and compass construction. Use a straightedge to draw a triangle that is *not* an equilateral triangle. Explain how you know.

(From Unit 1, Lesson 4.)

Lesson 4: Tables of Relative Frequencies

- Let's use tables to organize probabilities.

4.1: Notice and Wonder: Dog City

This two-way table summarizes data from a survey of 200 people who reported their home environment (urban or rural) and pet preference (dog or cat).

	urban	rural	total
cat	54	42	96
dog	80	24	104
total	134	66	200

What do you notice? What do you wonder?

4.2: Rolling into Tables

Decide which person will be partner A and which will be partner B.

The result of partner A's roll is represented by the values on the left side of the table. The result of partner B's roll is represented by the values on the top of the table.

Roll your number cube. Record the result of the roll. For example, if partner A rolls a 3 and partner B rolls a 5, then record 3,5. Repeat this process until your teacher tells you to stop.

Use the table to summarize the results. For example, if 6,6 appears on your list a total of five times, write a 5 in the bottom right cell of the table.

	1	2	3	4	5	6
1						
2						
3						
4						
5						
6						

1. Do the values in the table match your expectation? Explain your reasoning.

2. Based on the table, how many times did partner A roll a 5?

3. How many times did you both roll the same number?

4. What percentage of the rolls resulted in the same number from both partners?

5. What percentage of the rolls resulted in partner A rolling a 3 and partner B rolling a 6?

6. Based on the table, estimate the probability that partner A will roll a 2 and partner B will roll a 4. Explain your reasoning.

4.3: Traveling Methods

1. A company has an office in Austin, Texas, and an office in Copenhagen, Denmark. The company wants to know how employees get to work, so they take a survey of all the employees and summarize the results in a table.

	walk	car	public transit	bike	total
Austin	63	376	125	63	626
Copenhagen	48	67	95	267	477
total	111	443	220	330	1,103

a. If an employee is selected at random, what is the probability that they work in Austin and drive a car to work?

b. If an employee is selected at random, what is the probability that they work in Copenhagen and ride a bike to work?

c. If an employee is selected at random, what is the probability that they take public transit to work?

d. If an employee from Copenhagen is selected at random, what is the probability that they ride a bike to work?

e. If an employee who takes public transit to work is selected at random, what is the probability they work in Austin?

f. How are the last two questions different from the first three?

2. A school district is interested in how students get to school, so they survey their high school students to see how they get to school and separate the numbers by grade level. The results of the survey are summarized in the table.

	car	bus	other method	total
grade 9	1,141	3,196	228	4,565
grade 10	1,126	1,770	322	3,218
grade 11	1,732	799	133	2,664
grade 12	1,676	447	111	2,234
total	5,675	6,212	794	12,681

a. If a high school student is selected at random, what is the probability they are in grade 9 and ride the bus to school?

b. If a high school student is selected at random, what is the probability that they are in grade 12?

c. If a high school student is selected at random, what is the probability that they take a car to school?

d. If a grade 10 student is selected at random, what is the probability that they ride a bus to school?

e. If a grade 12 student is selected at random, what is the probability that they ride a bus to school?

f. If a student who rides the bus to school is selected at random, what is the probability that they are in grade 9?

Are you ready for more?

Clare surveyed 40 students at her school as part of a psychology project. Here are the two questions she asked:

- Do you like to swim? (Yes or No)

- What is your favorite season? (Winter, Spring, Summer, or Fall)

Here are the results of her survey.

	likes to swim	does not like to swim
winter	5	4
spring	8	3
summer	11	1
fall	4	4

1. Create a relative frequency table for Clare's data.

2. If a student that took Clare's survey is selected at random, what is the probability that they said they like to swim and their favorite season is summer?

3. Create two of your own survey questions or use Clare's questions to survey 20 or more people. Record your survey questions and display the results in a table.

4. Create a relative frequency table for your own data. What is the most common response to your survey? What is the least common response to your survey?

Lesson 4 Summary

Tables provide a useful structure for organizing data. When several responses have been collected about some categorical variables, the data can be organized into a frequency table. The table can be used to calculate relative frequencies, which can be interpreted as probabilities.

For example, 243 participants in a survey responded to questions about their favorite season and whether they like wearing pants or shorts better. The results are summarized in the table.

	pants	shorts
winter	21	16
spring	43	20
summer	18	56
autumn	40	29

This table can be turned into a relative frequency table by dividing each of the values in the cells by the total number of participants.

	pants	shorts
winter	0.09	0.07
spring	0.18	0.08
summer	0.07	0.23
autumn	0.16	0.12

If a person is randomly selected from among these 243 participants, we can see that the probability that the chosen person's favorite season is spring and likes shorts better than pants is 0.08. We can also use the fact that there were 63 people who listed spring as their favorite season ($43 + 20$), so the probability that a randomly selected person from this group likes spring best is around 0.26 ($\frac{63}{243} \approx 0.26$).

Lesson 4 Practice Problems

1. The table shows the results from a survey that asked 100 adults if they had a high school diploma and if their annual income was more than $30,000.

	$30,000 or less	more than $30,000
high school diploma	21	68
no high school diploma	9	2

A person who took the survey is selected at random.

   a. What is the probability that the person has a high school diploma and makes $30,000 or less?

   b. What is the probability that the person has no high school diploma and earns more than $30,000?

2. The table shows data from a science fair experiment that studied the number of eggs that hatched at three different temperatures.

	cool	room temperature	warm
hatched	6	14	23
not hatched	19	11	2

   a. What percentage of the eggs hatched?

   b. What percentage of the eggs that were at the cool temperature hatched?

   c. What percentage of the eggs were not at room temperature?

   d. What percentage of the eggs were at the warm temperature and did not hatch?

3. The table shows information from a survey about the resting heart rate in beats per minute (bpm), for 50 people living at altitudes above and below 10,000 feet.

	below 80 bpm	above 80 bpm	total
above 10,000 ft	3	19	22
10,000 ft or below	16	12	28
total	19	31	50

a. Create a two-way table that shows the relative frequency for each of the values in the table relative to all 50 people in the survey.

b. What is the probability that a person surveyed, selected at random, has a heart rate above 80 bpm or lives above 10,000 ft?

c. What is the probability that a person surveyed, selected at random, has a heart rate above 80 bpm and lives above 10,000 ft?

4. List all the possible outcomes for spinning the spinner and rolling a fair number cube.

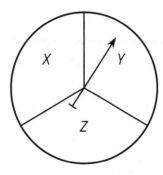

(From Unit 8, Lesson 3.)

5. A student flips a fair coin and then spins this spinner. How would you find the sample space?

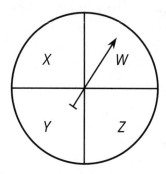

(From Unit 8, Lesson 3.)

6. Select **all** of the words for which the probability of selecting the letter A at random is $\frac{1}{4}$

   A. AREA

   B. ACID

   C. ANGRY

   D. APPEASED

   E. AARDVARK

(From Unit 8, Lesson 2.)

7. On an assignment, there are two multiple choice questions with four answers choices each. You have no idea what the correct answer is to either one so you guess.

    a. What is the probability that you get both of them right by guessing? Explain your answer.

    b. What is the probability that you get exactly one of them right by guessing? Explain your answer.

(From Unit 8, Lesson 1.)

8. Here are 2 circles. The smaller circle has radius r, circumference c, and diameter d. The larger circle has radius R, circumference C, and diameter D. The larger circle is a dilation of the smaller circle by a factor of k.

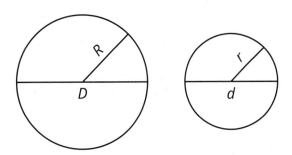

Using the circles, match the pairs of ratios with their values.

A. The ratios $\frac{C}{c}$ and $\frac{R}{r}$ are both equal to _____.

1. 2

2. k

B. The ratios $\frac{C}{D}$ and $\frac{c}{d}$ are both equal to _____.

3. π

C. The ratios $\frac{D}{R}$ and $\frac{d}{r}$ are both equal to _____.

(From Unit 7, Lesson 10.)

Lesson 5: Combining Events

Let's look at ways to describe events composed of other events.

5.1: Notice and Wonder: Birds and Bats

What do you notice? What do you wonder?

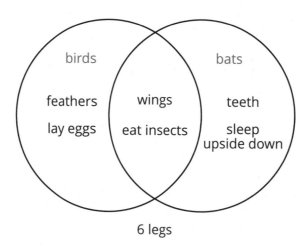

5.2: Eventful Islands

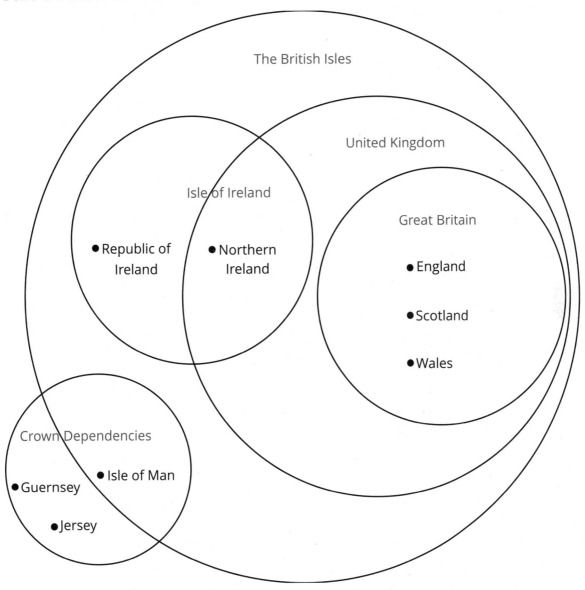

The small dots next to the names indicate that the name listed in the diagram is a country.

1. Based on the categories in the Venn diagram, describe Northern Ireland in a way that will not include any other countries.

2. Based on the categories in the Venn diagram, describe the Republic of Ireland in a way that will not include any other countries.

3. How many countries displayed are not part of The British Isles?

4. How many countries displayed are part of the United Kingdom?

5. How many countries displayed are part of the Island of Ireland?

6. How many places displayed are part of the United Kingdom and the Isle of Ireland?

7. How many places displayed are part of the United Kingdom or the Isle of Ireland?

8. If one of the crown dependencies (there are 3) is chosen at random, what is the probability that it is part of The British Isles?

9. Northern Ireland, England, Scotland and Wales are all part of the United Kingdom. If one of them is selected at random, what is the probability that it is also considered part of Great Britain?

10. Given that the Republic of Ireland, Northern Ireland, England, Scotland, Wales, and the Isle of Man are all part of The British Isles, what is the probability that one of them selected at random is part of the Island of Ireland?

5.3: Info Gap: College and Career Planning

Your teacher will give you either a problem card or a data card. Do not show or read your card to your partner.

If your teacher gives you the data card:

1. Silently read the information on your card.

2. Ask your partner "What specific information do you need?" and wait for your partner to ask for information. Only give information that is on your card. (Do not figure out anything for your partner!)

3. Before telling your partner the information, ask "Why do you need to know (that piece of information)?"

4. Read the problem card, and solve the problem independently.

5. Share the data card, and discuss your reasoning.

If your teacher gives you the problem card:

1. Silently read your card and think about what information you need to answer the question.

2. Ask your partner for the specific information that you need.

3. Explain to your partner how you are using the information to solve the problem.

4. When you have enough information, share the problem card with your partner, and solve the problem independently.

5. Read the data card, and discuss your reasoning.

5.4: Number Cube Descriptions

1. Roll two standard number cubes twenty times. Record your results in the table.

first cube	second cube

first cube	second cube

2. List all the possible outcomes in each event. The first one is done for you.

    a. The first cube is a 6. 6,1; 6,2; 6,3; 6,4; 6,5; 6,6

    b. The cubes have a 4 and a 6.

    c. The cubes are doubles. (Doubles means that the number on the two number cubes is the same.)

    d. The cubes are doubles and the first cube is a 6.

e. The cubes are doubles or the first cube is a 6.

f. The first cube is not a 6.

g. The cubes are doubles and the first cube is not a 6.

h. The cubes are not doubles.

3. Use the information in the table to answer the questions.

a. What percentage of the rolls have a 6 on the first cube?

b. What percentage of the rolls have a 4 and a 6?

c. What percentage of the rolls are doubles?

d. What percentage of the rolls are doubles and have a 6 on the first cube?

e. What percentage of the rolls are doubles or have a 6 on the first cube?

f. What percentage of the rolls do not have a 6 on the first cube?

g. What percentage of the rolls are doubles and do not have a 6 on the first cube?

h. What percentage of the rolls are not doubles?

4. The sample space has 36 outcomes. Use this and the number of outcomes in each event to find the actual probability for each event in the previous problem. Compare your answers.

5. Why is the actual probability different from the percentage of rolls you made for each event?

Are you ready for more?

1. Roll three standard number cubes forty times. Record your results in the table.

first cube	second cube	third cube	first cube	second cube	third cube

first cube	second cube	third cube	first cube	second cube	third cube

2. List all the possible outcomes in each event. The first one is done for you.

   a. The first cube is a 6. 661, 662, 663, 664, 665, 666, 651, 652, 653, 654, 655, 656, 641, 642, 643, 644, 645, 646, 631, 632, 633, 634, 635, 636, 621, 622, 623, 624, 625, 626, 611, 612, 613, 614, 615, 616

   b. The cubes have a 4, a 5, and a 6.

   c. The cubes are triples. (Triples means that the number on the three number cubes is the same.)

3. Use the information in the table to answer the questions.

   a. What percentage of the rolls have a 6 on the first cube?

   b. What percentage of the rolls have a 4, a 5, and a 6?

   c. What percentage of the rolls are triples?

4. The sample space has 216 outcomes. Use this and the number of outcomes in each event to find the actual probability for each event in the previous problem. Compare your answers.

5. If you rolled 500 times, do you think that the difference between the actual probability and the percentage of rolls you made for each event would increase or decrease? Explain your reasoning.

6. Describe a method for recording the 216 outcomes in the sample space. Do not actually record all 216 outcomes.

Lesson 5 Summary

In many cases, it is useful to talk about the important outcomes in a sample space by naming characteristics the outcomes share or characteristics that are not in the outcomes.

For example, consider a group of 12 first-year students in college and their choices of science courses.

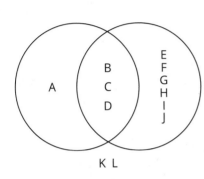

The circle on the left represents the students taking a chemistry class and the circle on the right represents the students taking a biology class. The region where the circles overlap represents the students taking both a chemistry class and a biology class. The students who are not included in either circle are not taking chemistry or biology.

We can describe some of the groups of students based on the characteristics they share or lack. For example:

- students A, B, C, and D are taking a chemistry course

- students A, K, and L are not taking a biology course

- students B, C, and D are taking a chemistry course and taking a biology course

- students E, F, G, H, I, and J are taking a biology course and are not taking a chemistry course

- students A, B, C, D, E, F, G, H, I, and J are taking a chemistry course or are taking a biology course

While listing the individual students in this case is not too difficult, when there are many outcomes in a sample space (which is often the case), it is often easier to describe the interesting ones using some characteristics they share.

Lesson 5 Practice Problems

1. 50 students were asked two survey questions:

   ○ Do you have a dog?

   ○ Do you have a cat?

   Their responses are summarized in the Venn diagram.

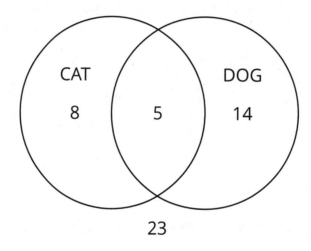

   a. How many students have a cat?

   b. How many students have a cat or a dog?

   c. How many students have a cat and a dog?

   d. How many students do not have a cat?

   e. How many students do not have a cat or a dog?

2. In the Venn diagram, the circle on the left represents all the whole numbers between 1 and 12 that are multiples of 2. The circle on the right represents all the numbers between 1 and 12 that are multiples of 3.

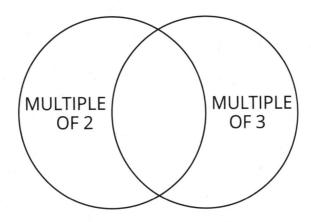

a. Which numbers are multiples of 2?

b. Which numbers are multiples of 3?

c. Which numbers belong in the region where the two circles overlap? Explain your reasoning.

d. Which whole numbers between 1 and 12 are not contained inside either circle in the Venn diagram?

e. What is the probability that a whole number between 1 and 12, selected at random, is a multiple of two or three?

f. What is the probability that a whole number between 1 and 12, selected at random, is not a multiple of 2?

3. Two classes of elementary school students are going on a field trip, and they will be provided with a snack. Each student selects one snack option. The table summarizes the snack preference of each student in the class.

	apple	carrot sticks	peach slices
class A	4	6	12
class B	7	3	14

a. What is the probability that a student selected at random prefers peach slices as a snack?

b. What is the probability that a student selected at random prefers an apple or carrot sticks as a snack?

c. What is the probability that a student in class A selected at random prefers an apple as a snack?

d. What is the probability that a student selected at random is in class B and prefers carrot sticks as a snack?

4. The table shows the results from a survey that asked 200 adults if they had a college diploma and if their annual income was more than $40,000.

	$40,000 or less	more than $40,000
college diploma	44	101
no college diploma	27	28

A person who took the survey is selected at random.

a. What is the probability that the person has a college diploma and makes $40,000 or less?

b. What is the probability that the person doesn't have a college diploma and earns more than $40,000?

(From Unit 8, Lesson 4.)

5. The table shows data from a science fair experiment that studied the average growth rate of 20 samples of fungus at 70 degrees Fahrenheit and 20 samples of fungus at 80 degrees Fahrenheit.

	70 degrees	80 degrees
above average growth rate	3	8
average growth rate	12	11
below average growth rate	5	1

a. What percentage of the samples had an above average growth rate?

b. What percentage of the samples at 70 degrees had an above average growth rate?

c. What percentage of the samples were at 80 degrees?

d. What percentage of the samples that had an average growth rate were at 80 degrees?

(From Unit 8, Lesson 4.)

6. Here is a central angle that measures 1.5 radians.

Select the statement that *must* be true.

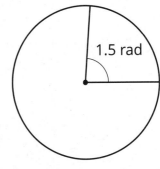

A. The area of the whole circle is 1.5 times the area of the slice.

B. The circumference of the whole circle is 1.5 times the length of the arc formed by the angle.

C. The length of the arc defined by the angle is 1.5 times longer than the radius.

D. The length of the arc is 1.5π units.

(From Unit 7, Lesson 11.)

Lesson 6: The Addition Rule

- Let's learn about and use the addition rule.

6.1: Hats Off, Sneakers On

The table displays information about people at a neighborhood park.

	wearing sneakers	not wearing sneakers	total
wearing a hat	8	2	10
not wearing a hat	3	12	15
total	11	14	25

1. Andre says the number of people wearing sneakers or wearing a hat is 21, because there are a total of 10 people wearing a hat and a total of 11 people wearing sneakers. Is Andre correct? Explain your reasoning.

2. What is the probability that a person selected at random from those in the park is wearing sneakers or wearing a hat?

6.2: State Names

Jada has a way to find the probability of a random outcome being in event A or event B. She says, "We use the probability of the outcome being in event A, then add the probability of the outcome being in category B. Now some outcomes have been counted twice, so we have to subtract the probability of the outcome being in both events so that those outcomes are only counted once."

Jada's method can be rewritten as:

$$P(\text{A or B}) = P(\text{A}) + P(\text{B}) - P(\text{A and B})$$

1. The table of data summarizes information about the 50 states in the United States from a census in the year 2000. A state is chosen at random from the list of 50. Let event A be "the state name begins with A through M" and event B be "the population of the state is less than 4 million."

	population less than 4 million	population at least 4 million
name begins with A through M	11	15
name begins with N through Z	13	11

Alaska is one of the 11 states in the top left cell of the table. California is one of the 15 states in the top right cell of the table. Nebraska is one of the 13 states in the bottom left cell of the table. New York is one of the 11 states in the bottom right cell of the table. For each event, write which of the four states listed here is an outcome in that event.

   a. A or B

   b. A

   c. B

   d. A and B

2. Find each of the probabilities when a state is chosen at random:
   a. $P(\text{A or B})$

b. $P(A)$

c. $P(B)$

d. $P(A \text{ and } B)$

3. Does Jada's formula work for these events? Show your reasoning.

4. Seniors at a high school are allowed to go off campus for lunch if they have a grade of A in all their classes or perfect attendance. An assistant principal in charge of academics knows that the probability of a randomly selected senior having A's in all their classes is 0.1. An assistant principal in charge of attendance knows that the probability of a randomly selected senior having perfect attendance is 0.16. The cafeteria staff know that the probability of a randomly selected senior being allowed to go off campus for lunch is 0.18. Use Jada's formula to find the probability that a randomly selected senior has all As and perfect attendance.

Are you ready for more?

Priya lists all of the multiples of 3 for whole numbers between 1 and 48 inclusive.

3, 6, 9, 12, 15, 18, 21, 24, 27, 30, 33, 36, 39, 42, 45, 48

Tyler lists the all of the multiples of 4 between 1 and 48 inclusive.

4, 8, 12, 16, 20, 24, 28, 32, 36, 40, 44, 48

1. Use a Venn diagram to display the multiples of 3 and the multiples of 4 between 1 and 48.

2. If a whole number between 1 and 48 inclusive is selected at random, find each probability:
   a. $P(\text{multiple of } 3)$

   b. $P(\text{multiple of } 4)$

   c. $P(\text{multiple of } 3 \text{ or } 4)$

   d. $P(\text{multiple of } 3 \text{ and } 4)$

3. Priya and Tyler extend their lists of multiples to include whole numbers between 1 and 96 inclusive. If a whole number between 1 and 96 inclusive is selected at random, find each probability and compare it to the probability in the previous problem:
   a. $P(\text{multiple of } 3)$

   b. $P(\text{multiple of } 4)$

   c. $P(\text{multiple of } 3 \text{ or } 4)$

   d. $P(\text{multiple of } 3 \text{ and } 4)$

4. If a whole number between 1 and 100 inclusive is selected at random, what do you think $P(\text{multiple of } 3 \text{ and } 4)$ is? Explain your reasoning.

5. If a whole number between 1 and n, inclusive, for any whole number value of n, what is $P(\text{multiple of } 3 \text{ and } 4)$?

6.3: Coffee or Juice?

1. At a cafe, customers order coffee at the bar, and then either go to another table where the cream and sugar are kept, or find a seat. Based on observations, a worker estimates that 70% of customers go to the second table for cream or sugar. The worker also observes that about 60% of all customers use cream for their coffee and 50% of all customers use sugar. Use the worker's estimates to find the percentage of all customers who use both cream and sugar for their coffee. Explain or show your reasoning.

2. At the grocery store, 70% of the different types of juice come in a bottle holding at least 400 milliliters (mL) and 40% of the different types of juice come in a low-sugar version. Only 25% of the juice varieties are in bottles holding at least 400 mL and have a low-sugar version. What percentage of the different types of juice come in a bottle holding at least 400 mL or are low-sugar? Explain your reasoning.

3. Complete the table showing the number of cans and bottles of low-sugar and regular juice in one of the shelves at a grocery store. You may not use zero in any of the empty spaces.

	less than 400 mL	at least 400 mL	total
low-sugar available			80
no low-sugar available			
total	60	140	

Use the table to find the probabilities for a juice chosen from the shelf at random.

a. P(less than 400 mL)

b. P(no low-sugar available)

c. P(no low-sugar available or less than 400 mL)

d. P(no low-sugar available and less than 400 mL)

Lesson 6 Summary

The **addition rule** is used to compute probabilities of compound events. The addition rule states that, given events A and B, $P(A \text{ or } B) = P(A) + P(B) - P(A \text{ and } B)$.

For example, the student council sold 100 shirts that are either gray or blue and in sizes medium and large.

	medium	large	total
gray	20	10	30
blue	15	55	70
total	35	65	100

A student who bought a shirt is chosen at random. One way to find the probability that this student bought a shirt that is blue or medium is to begin with the probabilities for shirts sold in that color and size. The probability that the student bought a blue shirt is 0.70 since 70 out of the 100 shirts sold were blue. The probability that the student bought a medium shirt is 0.35 since 35 out of the 100 shirts sold were medium.

Because we are interested in the probability of a blue shirt or a medium shirt being purchased, we might think we should add these probabilities together to find $0.70 + 0.35 = 1.05$.

This doesn't seem to work since it is saying the probability is greater than 1.

The problem is that the 15 students who bought shirts that are both medium in size and blue are counted twice when we do this. To fix this double counting, we should subtract the probability that the chosen student is in both categories so that these students are only counted once.

The addition rule then shows that the probability the student bought a medium shirt or a blue shirt is 0.90 since $P(\text{small or white}) = P(\text{small}) + P(\text{white}) - P(\text{small and white})$ or $P(\text{small or white}) = 0.35 + 0.70 - 0.15$, which is 0.90.

Glossary
- addition rule

Lesson 6 Practice Problems

1. The table displays the number and type of tickets bought for a play that was performed in both the afternoon and evening.

	child ticket	adult ticket
afternoon	36	127
evening	12	188

The addition rule states that given events A and B,

$P(A \text{ or } B) = P(A) + P(B) - P(A \text{ and } B)$. Show how to apply the addition rule for the events "a child ticket is bought for a play" and "the play is performed in the afternoon."

2. A biologist studies two different invasive species, purple loosestrife and the common reed, at sites in both wetland and coastal habitats. Purple loosestrife is present in 35% of the sites. Common reed is present in 55% of the sites. Both purple loosestrife and common reed are present in 23% of the sites. What percentage of the sites have purple loosestrife or common reed present?

A. 12%

B. 22%

C. 67%

D. 90%

3. 30 teachers and students participate in a student-faculty basketball game as a fundraiser. They are surveyed after the game by the sports medicine class to find out how many of them stretched before the game. The results of the survey are shown in the table.

	younger than 18 years old	18–30 years old	more than 30 years old
stretched before the game	5	9	4
did not stretch before the game	10	1	1

One of the sports medicine students, Han, wants to know the probability that one of the participants in the game selected at random is younger than 18 years old or stretched before the game. To figure this out, he adds the three values in the first row of the table (5, 9, and 4) to the two values listed under the heading "younger than 18 years old" (5 and 10). He then divides that answer by 30 and obtains a probability of $\frac{33}{30}$. Han realizes that $\frac{33}{30}$ is greater than 1 and determines that he must have made a mistake.

a. What is Han's mistake? Explain your reasoning.

b. How does the addition rule account for this kind of mistake?

4. Two classes of elementary school students were asked what activity they want to do during recess. Each student selects one recess option. The table summarizes the recess preference of each student in the class.

	tag	playground	kickball
class A	2	7	9
class B	7	10	5

a. What is the probability that a student selected at random prefers to play tag at recess?

b. What is the probability that a student selected at random prefers to play tag or kickball at recess?

c. What is the probability that a student in class A selected at random prefers to play kickball at recess?

d. What is the probability that a student selected at random is in class B and prefers to play tag at recess?

(From Unit 8, Lesson 5.)

5. A student picks a random letter from the word "dog" and a random letter from the word "barks."

a. How many outcomes are in the sample space?

b. What is the probability that an "o" is chosen?

c. What is the probability that a "k" is chosen?

d. What is the probability that a "o" and a "k" are chosen?

(From Unit 8, Lesson 3.)

6. The table shows information from a survey about the resting heart rate in beats per minute (bpm), for 200 college students who are in the marching band and who are not in the marching band.

	below 80 bpm	above 80 bpm	total
in the marching band	56	28	84
not in the marching band	66	50	116
total	122	78	200

a. Create a two-way table that shows the relative frequency for each of the values in the table relative to all 200 people in the survey.

b. What is the probability that a person surveyed, selected at random, has a heart rate above 80 bpm or is in the marching band?

c. What is the probability that a person surveyed, selected at random, has a heart rate below 80 bpm and is not in the marching band?

(From Unit 8, Lesson 4.)

7. The circle in the image has been divided into congruent sectors. What is the measure of the central angle of the shaded region in radians?

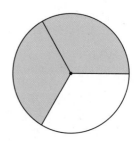

(From Unit 7, Lesson 12.)

Lesson 7: Related Events

- Let's see how events are related.

7.1: Drawing Crayons

A bag contains 1 crayon of each color: red, orange, yellow, green, blue, pink, maroon, and purple.

1. A person chooses a crayon at random out of the bag, uses it for a bit, then puts it back in the bag. A second person comes to get a crayon chosen at random out of the bag. What is the probability the second person gets the yellow crayon?

2. A person chooses a crayon at random out of the bag and walks off to use it. A second person comes to get a crayon chosen at random out of the bag. What is the probability the second person gets the yellow crayon?

7.2: Choosing Doors

1. On a game show, a contestant is presented with 3 doors. One of the doors hides a prize and the other two doors have nothing behind them.
   - The contestant chooses one of the doors by number.

   - The host, knowing where the prize is, reveals one of the empty doors that the contestant did not choose.

   - The host then offers the contestant a chance to stay with the door they originally chose or to switch to the remaining door.

   - The final chosen door is opened to reveal whether the contestant has won the prize.

   Choose one partner to play the role of the host and the other to be the contestant. The host should think of a number: 1, 2, or 3 to represent the prize door. Play the game keeping track of whether the contestant stayed with their original door or switched and whether the contestant won or lost.

Switch roles so that the other person is the host and play again. Continue playing the game until the teacher tells you to stop. Use the table to record your results.

	stay	switch	total
win			
lose			
total			

a. Based on your table, if a contestant decides they will choose to stay with their original choice, what is the probability they will win the game?

b. Based on your table, if a contestant decides they will choose to switch their choice, what is the probability they will win the game?

c. Are the two probabilities the same?

2. In another version of the game, the host forgets which door hides the prize. The game is played in a similar way, but sometimes the host reveals the prize and the game immediately ends with the player losing, since it does not matter whether the contestant stays or switches.

Choose one partner to play the role of the host and the other to be the contestant. The contestant should choose a number: 1, 2, or 3. The host should choose one of the other two numbers. The contestant can choose to stay with their original number or switch to the last number.

After following these steps, roll the number cube to see which door contains the prize:

○ Rolling 1 or 4 means the prize was behind door 1.

○ Rolling 2 or 5 means the prize was behind door 2.

○ Rolling 3 or 6 means the prize was behind door 3.

Play the game keeping track of whether the contestant stayed with their original door or switched and whether the contestant won or lost.

Switch roles so that the other person is the host and play again. Continue playing the game until the teacher tells you to stop. Use the table to record your results.

	stay	switch	total
win			
lose			
total			

a. Based on your table, if a contestant decides they will choose to stay with their original choice, what is the probability they will win the game?

b. Based on your table, if a contestant decides they will choose to switch with their original choice, what is the probability they will win the game?

c. Are the two probabilities the same?

Are you ready for more?

In another version of the game, the contestant is presented with 5 doors. One of the doors hides a prize and the other four doors have nothing behind them.

- The contestant chooses 3 doors by number.

- The host, knowing where the prize is, reveals 3 of the doors that have nothing behind them. Two of the doors that the contestant has chosen that are empty and one of the other doors that are empty.

- The host then offers the contestant a chance to stay with the door they originally chose or to switch to the remaining door.

- The final chosen door is opened to reveal whether the contestant has won the prize.

Choose one partner to play the role of the host and the other to be the contestant. The host should think of a number: 1, 2, 3, 4, or 5 to represent the prize door. Play the game keeping track of whether the contestant stayed with their original door or switched and whether the contestant won or lost.

Switch roles so that the other person is the host and play again. Continue playing the game until the teacher tells you to stop. Use the table to record your results.

	stay	switch	total
win			
lose			
total			

1. Based on your table, if a contestant decides they will choose to stay with their original choice, what is the probability they will win the game?

2. Based on your table, if a contestant decides they will choose to switch with their original choice, what is the probability they will win the game?

3. Are the two probabilities the same?

Lesson 7 Summary

When considering probabilities for two events it is useful to know whether the events are independent or dependent. **Independent events** are two events from the same experiment for which the probability of one event is not affected by whether the other event occurs or not. **Dependent events** are two events from the same experiment for which the probability of one event *is* affected by whether the other event occurs or not.

For example, let's say a bag contains 3 green blocks and 2 blue blocks. You are going to take two blocks out of the bag.

Consider two experiments:

1. Take a block out, write down the color, return the block to the bag, and then choose a second block. The event, "the second block is green" is independent of the event, "the first block is blue." Since the first block is replaced, it doesn't matter what block you picked the first time when you pick a second block.

2. Take a block out, hold on to it, then take another block out. The same two events, "the second block is green" and "the first block is blue," are dependent.

If you get a blue block on the first draw, then the bag has 3 green blocks and 1 blue block in it, so $P(\text{green}) = \frac{3}{4}$.

If you get a green block on the first draw, then the bag has 2 green blocks and 2 blue blocks in it, so $P(\text{green}) = \frac{1}{2}$.

Since the probability of getting a green block on the second draw changes depending on whether the event of drawing a blue block on the first draw occurs or not, the two events are dependent.

In some cases, it is difficult to know whether events are independent without collecting some data. For example, a basketball player shoots two free throws. Does the probability of making the second shot depend on the outcome of the first shot? Some data would need to be collected about how often the player makes the second shot overall and how often the player makes the second shot after making the first so that you could compare the estimated probabilities.

Glossary

- dependent events
- independent events

Lesson 7 Practice Problems

1. Each of the letters A through J are printed on tiles that are placed in a hat. Andre selects a tile at random and then replaces it. Clare then selects a tile at random.

    a. What is the probability that Andre selects a tile labeled B?

    b. What is the probability that Clare selects a tile labeled B?

    c. What is the probability that both Andre and Clare select a tile labeled B?

    d. Are the events of Andre selecting a tile and Clare selecting a tile dependent or independent? Explain your reasoning.

2. The Bulldogs have won approximately 67% of their 30 baseball games this season. The Bulldogs won 9 of the 10 games they played when Diego was the starting pitcher. Are the events "the Bulldogs win the game" and "the Bulldogs win the game when Diego is the starting pitcher" dependent or independent events? Explain your reasoning.

3. Describe two events that are independent. Explain your reasoning.

Geometry

4. The table displays the number and type of tickets bought for a baseball tournament held on a Saturday and Sunday.

	child ticket	adult ticket
Saturday	27	41
Sunday	14	29

The addition rule states that given events A and B,
$P(A \text{ or } B) = P(A) + P(B) - P(A \text{ and } B)$. Show how to apply the addition rule for the events "a child ticket is bought for a baseball tournament" and "the day of the tournament is Sunday."

(From Unit 8, Lesson 6.)

5. A researcher surveys 200 randomly selected college students to determine the number of education majors and mathematics majors. 16% of the students surveyed are education majors and 6% of the students surveyed are mathematics majors. 2% of the students are both education majors and mathematics majors. What percentage of the students surveyed are education majors or mathematics majors?

A. 2%

B. 20%

C. 22%

D. 24%

(From Unit 8, Lesson 6.)

6. 100 students were asked two survey questions:

- Do you have a garden?

- Are you a gamer?

Their responses are summarized in the Venn diagram.

How many students surveyed have a garden?

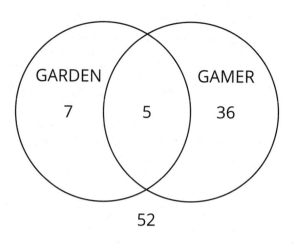

A. 5

B. 7

C. 12

D. 36

(From Unit 8, Lesson 5.)

7. The table shows the preferences of 40 students surveyed about the design of a new t-shirt for students who are graduating this year.

	short sleeves	long sleeves
pink	12	5
black	14	9

What is the probability that a student surveyed, selected at random, preferred a pink t-shirt with long sleeves?

(From Unit 8, Lesson 4.)

8. Write a formula that could be used to find the area of this sector.

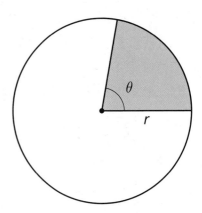

(From Unit 7, Lesson 13.)

9. *Technology required.* Find the missing measurements in triangle *ABC*.

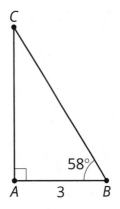

(From Unit 4, Lesson 7.)

Lesson 8: Conditional Probability

- Let's examine conditional probability.

8.1: She Made Some Tarts

1. Noah will select 1 card at random from a standard deck of cards. Find the probabilities. Explain or show your reasoning.

   a. P(the card is a queen)

   b. P(the card is a heart)

   c. P(the card is a queen and heart)

2. Elena pulls out only the hearts from the deck and sets the rest of the cards aside. She shuffles the hearts and draws one card. What is the probability she gets a queen?

8.2: Under One Condition

Kiran notices that the probabilities from the warm-up can be arranged into at least two equations.

P(the card is a queen and heart) $= P$(the card is a queen | the card is a heart) $\cdot P$(the card is a heart) since $\frac{1}{52} = \frac{1}{13} \cdot \frac{13}{52}$.

P(the card is a queen and heart) $= P$(the card is a heart | the card is a queen) $\cdot P$(the card is a queen) since $\frac{1}{52} = \frac{1}{4} \cdot \frac{4}{52}$.

Kiran wonders if it is always true that $P(A \text{ and } B) = P(A \mid B) \cdot P(B)$ for events A and B. He wants to check additional examples from drawing a card from a deck.

1. If Event A is "the card is black" and Event B is "the card is a king," does the equation hold? Explain or show your reasoning.

2. If Event A is "the card is a face card" and Event B is "the card is a spade," does the equation hold? Explain or show your reasoning.

8.3: Coin and Cube

A coin is flipped, then a standard number cube is rolled. Let A represent the event "the coin lands showing heads" and B represent "the standard number cube lands showing 4."

1. Are events A and B independent or dependent? Explain your reasoning.

2. Find the probabilities
    a. $P(A)$

    b. $P(B)$

    c. $P(A \mid B)$

    d. $P(B \mid A)$

3. Describe the meaning of the events "not A" and "not B" in this situation, then find the probabilities.
    a. $P(A \mid \text{not } B)$

    b. $P(B \mid \text{not } A)$

4. Are any of the probabilities the same? Is there a relationship between those situations? Explain your reasoning.

Are you ready for more?

Students are writing programs in their robotics class using two different programming languages that are very similar. 70% of the programs are written in the first programming language and the other 30% percent are written in the second programming language. The newer robots only accept programs written in the first programming language and the older robots only accept programs written in the second programming language.

In this robotics class, Andre's job is to determine which programming language each program is written in. He determines the programming language correctly 90% of the time for each of the programs. If Andre determines that a program is written in the second programming language, what is the probability that the program is actually written in the first programming language? Explain your reasoning.

Lesson 8 Summary

A **conditional probability** is the probability that one event occurs under the condition that another event occurs.

For example, we will remove two marbles from a jar that contains 3 green marbles, 2 blue marbles, 1 white marble, and 1 black marble. We might consider the conditional probability that the second marble we remove is green given that the first marble removed was green. The notation for this probability is $P(\text{green second} \mid \text{green first})$ where the vertical line can be read as "under the condition that the next event occurs" or "given that the next event occurs." In this example, $P(\text{green second} \mid \text{green first}) = \frac{2}{6}$ since we assume the condition that the first marble drawn was green has happened, so the second draw only has 2 possible green marbles left to draw out of 6 marbles still in the jar.

To find the probability of two events happening together, we can use a multiplication rule:

$$P(A \text{ and } B) = P(A \mid B) \cdot P(B)$$

For example, to find the probability that we draw two green marbles from the jar, we could write out the entire sample space and find the probability from that or we could use this rule.

P(green second and green first) $= P$(green second | green first) $\cdot P$(green first)

Since the probability of getting green on the first draw is $\frac{3}{7}$ and the conditional probability was considered previously, we can find the probability that both events occur using the multiplication rule.

P(green second and green first) $= \frac{2}{6} \cdot \frac{3}{7}$ This tells us that the probability of getting green marbles in both draws is $\frac{1}{7}$ (since this is equivalent to $\frac{6}{42}$).

In cases where events A and B are independent, $P(A \mid B) = P(A)$ since the probability does not change whether B occurs or not. In these cases, the multiplication rule becomes:

$P(A \text{ and } B) = P(A) \cdot P(B)$

For example, when flipping a coin and rolling a standard number cube, the events "getting a tails for the coin" and "getting 5 for the number cube" are independent. That means we can find the probability of both events occurring to be $\frac{1}{12}$ by using the multiplication rule

P(heads and 5) $= \frac{1}{2} \cdot \frac{1}{6}$

Glossary

- conditional probability

Lesson 8 Practice Problems

1. Jada rolls one standard number cube, then she rolls another standard number cube.

    a. What is the probability that she rolls a 5 on both number cubes?

    b. What is the probability that the second roll is a 5 under the condition that the first roll is a 6?

    c. What is the probability that the second roll is a 5 under the condition that the first roll is a 5?

    d. What is the probability that the second roll is not a 5?

    e. What is the probability that the first roll is a 5 and the second roll is not a 5?

2. There are four slices of pizza left to choose from. Each slice of pizza has one topping. Three of the slices have sausage as a topping and the fourth slice has pepperoni as a topping. Kiran randomly selects one slice then Mai randomly selects one slice. What is the probability that Mai selects a slice of pepperoni pizza under the condition that Kiran selects a slice of sausage pizza?

    A. $\frac{1}{3}$

    B. $\frac{1}{4}$

    C. $\frac{2}{3}$

    D. $\frac{2}{4}$

3. Han's soccer team plays a soccer game in the morning. Lin's soccer team plays a soccer game in the afternoon against a different team than Han's soccer team played in the morning. Let A represent the event "Han's soccer team wins the morning game" and B represent the event "Lin's soccer team wins the afternoon game."

    a. Describe the meaning of $P(B \mid A)$.

    b. Do you think A and B are independent events? Explain your reasoning.

    c. If the events are independent, how are $P(B \mid A)$ and $P(B)$ related?

4. Each of the letters A through F are written on slips of paper and placed in a hat. Priya selects a slip of paper at random and then replaces it. Noah then selects a slip of paper at random.

    a. What is the probability that Priya selects a slip of paper labeled A?

    b. What is the probability that Noah selects a slip of paper labeled A?

    c. What is the probability that both Priya and Noah select a paper labeled A?

    d. Are the events of Priya selecting a paper and Noah selecting a paper dependent or independent? Explain your reasoning.

(From Unit 8, Lesson 7.)

5. The Wildcats have won approximately 80% of their 20 basketball games this season. The Wildcats won 5 of the 8 games they played when Elena started the game. Are the events "the Wildcats win the game" and "the Wildcats win the game when Elena started the game" dependent or independent events? Explain your reasoning.

(From Unit 8, Lesson 7.)

6. In a genetics experiment on plants, 17% of the plants exhibit trait A and 22% of the plants exhibit trait B. 36% of the plants exhibit trait A or trait B. What percentage of the plants exhibit both trait A and trait B?

(From Unit 8, Lesson 6.)

7. 70 students were asked two survey questions:

- Do you play a school sport?

- Are you a member of the school choir?

Their responses are summarized in the Venn diagram.

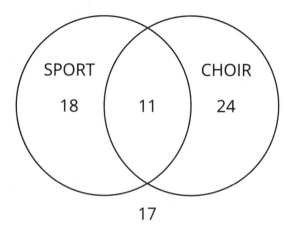

a. How many students play a school sport?

b. How many students play a school sport or are a member of the school choir?

c. How many students play a school sport and are a member of the school choir?

d. How many students are not a member of the school choir?

e. Name two ways to determine how many students play a sport.

(From Unit 8, Lesson 5.)

Lesson 9: Using Tables for Conditional Probability

- Let's use tables to estimate conditional probabilities.

9.1: Math Talk: Fractions in Fractions

Evaluate each expression mentally.

$$\frac{7}{11} \div \frac{8}{11}$$

$$\frac{\left(\frac{1}{3}\right)}{\left(\frac{2}{3}\right)}$$

$$\frac{\left(\frac{1}{4}\right)}{\left(\frac{1}{2}\right)}$$

$$\frac{\left(\frac{3}{8}\right)\left(\frac{8}{19}\right)}{\left(\frac{5}{19}\right)}$$

9.2: A Possible Cure

A pharmaceutical company is testing a new medicine for a disease using 115 test subjects. Some of the test subjects are given the new medicine and others are given a placebo. The results of their tests are summarized in the table.

	no more symptoms	symptoms persist	total
given medicine	31	26	57
given placebo	16	42	58
total	47	68	115

1. Divide the value in each cell by the total number of test subjects to find each probability to two decimal places. Some of the values have been completed for you.

	no more symptoms	symptoms persist	total
given medicine	0.27		0.50
given placebo			
total			1

If one of these test subjects is selected at random, find each probability:

   a. P(symptoms persist)

   b. P(given medicine and symptoms persist)

   c. P(given placebo or symptoms persist)

2. From the original table, divide each cell by the total for the row to find the probabilities with row conditions. Some of the values have been completed for you.

	no more symptoms	symptoms persist	total
given medicine	0.54		
given placebo			1

    a. P(symptoms persist | given medicine)

    b. P(no more symptoms | given placebo)

3. Jada didn't read the instructions for the previous problem well and used the table she created on the first problem to divide each cell by the probability total for each row. For example, in the top left cell she calculated $0.27 \div 0.5$. Complete the table using Jada's method.

	no more symptoms	symptoms persist	total
given medicine			
given placebo			

What do you notice about this table?

4. From the original table, divide each cell by the total for the column to find the probabilities with column conditions. Some of the values have been completed for you.

	no more symptoms	symptoms persist
given medicine	0.66	
given placebo		
total		1

    a. P(given medicine | symptoms persist)

    b. P(given placebo | no more symptoms)

5. Are the events "symptoms persist" and "given medicine" independent events? Explain or show your reasoning.

6. Based on your work, does being given this medicine have an impact on whether symptoms persist or not?

Are you ready for more?

Consider the data collected from all students in grades 11 and 12 and their intentions of going to prom.

	going to prom	not going to prom	total
grade 11	43	84	127
grade 12	81	35	116
total	124	119	243

1. $\frac{124}{243}$ of the students and grade 11 and 12 reported that they are going to prom and $\frac{119}{243}$ of them reported that they are not going to prom. Fill in the table so the the fraction of students in grade 11 reporting that they are going to prom is $\frac{124}{243}$ and the number of students in grade 12 reporting that they are going to prom is $\frac{119}{243}$. You may use non-integer values rounded to the nearest hundredth.

	going to prom	not going to prom	total
grade 11			127
grade 12			116
total	124	119	243

2. Based on your results from the previous problem, is there any possibility that the events of a student's grade level and whether or not they are going to prom could be independent events? Explain your reasoning.

9.3: The Blood Bank

A blood bank in a region has some information about the blood types of people in its community. Blood types are grouped into type O, A, B, and AB. Each blood type either has the Rh factor (Rh+) or not (Rh-). If a person is randomly selected from the community, the probability of their having each blood type and Rh factor combination is shown in the table.

	O	A	B	AB
Rh+	0.374	0.357	0.085	0.034
Rh-	0.066	0.063	0.015	0.006

1. What does the 0.085 in the table represent?

2. Use the table or create additional tables to find the probabilities, then describe the meaning of the event.

   a. $P(O)$

   b. $P(Rh+)$

   c. $P(O \text{ and } Rh+)$

   d. $P(O \text{ or } Rh+)$

   e. $P(O \mid Rh+)$

   f. $P(Rh+ \mid O)$

Lesson 9 Summary

Organizing data in tables is a useful way to see information and compute probabilities. Consider the data collected from all students in grades 11 and 12 and their intentions of going to prom.

	going to prom	not going to prom	total
grade 11	43	84	127
grade 12	81	35	116
total	124	119	243

A student is randomly selected from this group of students. We can find a number of probabilities based on the table.

$P(\text{grade 12 and going to prom}) = \frac{81}{243}$ since there are 81 students who are both in 12th grade and going to prom out of all 243 students in the group who could be selected.

$P(\text{grade 12}) = \frac{116}{243}$ since there are 116 grade 12 students out of the entire group.

$P(\text{going to prom}) = \frac{124}{243}$ since there are 124 students going to prom out of the entire group.

$P(\text{grade 12 or going to prom}) = \frac{159}{243}$ since there are 159 students in grade 12 or going to prom (43 from grade 11 going to prom, 81 from grade 12 going to prom, and 35 from grade 12 not going to prom).

$P(\text{going to prom} \mid \text{grade 12}) = \frac{81}{116}$ represents the probability that the chosen student is going to prom under the condition that they are in grade 12. The group we are considering is different for this probability since the condition is that they are in grade 12. Imagine all grade 12 students are in a room and we are only selecting from this group. Therefore 81 students are going to prom from this group out of 116 students in the group.

$P(\text{grade 11} \mid \text{going to prom}) = \frac{43}{124}$ represents the probability that the chosen student is in grade 11 under the condition that they are going to prom. In this case, we imagine that everyone going to prom is gathered in a room and we are selecting one student from this group. The probability that this student is in grade 11 when just considering this group is $\frac{43}{124}$.

The last two probabilities can also be found using the multiplication rule.

$P(\text{A and B}) = P(\text{A} \mid \text{B}) \cdot P(\text{B})$ can be rewritten $P(\text{A} \mid \text{B}) = \frac{P(\text{A and B})}{P(\text{B})}$

For example, substituting values into

$P(\text{going to prom} \mid \text{grade 12}) = \frac{P(\text{going to prom and grade 12})}{P(\text{grade 12})}$ gives $\frac{81}{116} = \frac{\left(\frac{81}{243}\right)}{\left(\frac{116}{243}\right)}$ which is a true

equation.

Lesson 9 Practice Problems

1. A tour company makes trips to see dolphins in the morning and in the afternoon. The two-way table summarizes whether or not customers saw dolphins on a total of 40 different trips.

	morning	afternoon
dolphins	19	14
no dolphins	3	4

   a. If a trip is selected at random, what is the probability that customers did not see dolphins on that trip?

   b. If a trip is selected at random, what is the probability that customers did not see dolphins under the condition that the trip was in the morning?

   c. Are the events of seeing dolphins and the time of the trip (morning or afternoon) dependent or independent events? Explain your reasoning.

2. Noah is unsure whether the coin and number cube he has are fair. He flips the coin then rolls the number cube and records the result. He does this a total of 50 times. The results are summarized in the table.

	one	two	three	four	five	six
heads	5	3	5	3	5	6
tails	3	4	5	2	6	3

   a. Create a two-way table that displays the probability for each outcome based on Noah's tests.

   b. If one of Noah's 50 results is selected at random, what is the probability that the coin was heads?

   c. If one of Noah's 50 results is selected at random, what is the probability that the number cube was 5?

3. A student surveys 30 people as part of a project for a statistics class. Here are the survey questions.

   ○ Are you left-handed or right-handed?

   ○ Are you left-eye dominant or right-eye dominant?

The results of the survey are summarized in the two-way table.

	right-eye dominant	left-eye dominant
right-handed	14	11
left-handed	3	2

What is the probability that a person from the survey chosen at random is right-handed under the condition that they are right-eye dominant?

   A. $\frac{25}{30}$

   B. $\frac{14}{30}$

   C. $\frac{14}{25}$

   D. $\frac{14}{17}$

4. Priya flips a fair coin and then rolls a standard number cube. What is the probability that she rolled a 3 under the condition that she flipped heads?

   A. $\frac{1}{2}$

   B. $\frac{1}{6}$

   C. $\frac{1}{12}$

   D. $\frac{3}{12}$

(From Unit 8, Lesson 8.)

5. Andre flips one fair coin and then flips another fair coin.

    a. What is the probability that he gets heads on both coins?

    b. What is the probability that he gets heads on the second coin under the condition that the first flip is heads?

    c. What is the probability that the second flip is not heads?

    d. What is the probability that the first flip is heads and the second flip is not heads?

(From Unit 8, Lesson 8.)

6. Han randomly selects a card from a standard deck of cards. He places it on his desk and then Jada randomly selects a card from the remaining cards in the same deck.

    a. What is the probability that Han selects a card that has diamonds on it?

    b. What is the probability that Jada selects a card that has diamonds on it?

    c. What is the probability that Han selects a card that has diamonds on it and that Jada selects a card that has diamonds on it?

    d. Are the events of Han and Jada randomly selecting a card dependent or independent? Explain your reasoning.

(From Unit 8, Lesson 7.)

7. An agriculturist takes 50 samples of soil and measures the levels of two nutrients, nitrogen and phosphorus. In 46% of the samples the nitrogen levels are low and in 28% of the samples the phosphorus levels are low. In 10% of the samples both the nitrogen and the phosphorus levels are low. What percentage of the samples have nitrogen levels or phosphorus levels that are low?

(From Unit 8, Lesson 6.)

8. Select **all** of the situations that have a 50% chance of occurring.

   A. Rolling a standard number cube and getting a 3.

   B. Flipping two fair coins and getting heads on exactly one of the flips.

   C. Picking a letter at random from the word SEED and getting an E.

   D. Picking a letter at random from the word ORCHID and getting a vowel.

   E. Getting the answer correct when guessing randomly on a true or false question.

   (From Unit 8, Lesson 1.)

9. A solid has volume 6 cubic units and surface area 14 square units. The solid is dilated, and the image has surface area 224 square units. What is the volume of the image?

   (From Unit 5, Lesson 8.)

Lesson 10: Using Probability to Determine Whether Events Are Independent

- Let's take a closer look at dependent and independent events.

10.1: Which One Doesn't Belong: Events

A coin is flipped and a standard number cube is rolled. Which one doesn't belong?

Set 1

Event A1: the coin landing heads up

Event B1: rolling a 3 or 5

Set 3

Event A3: rolling a prime number

Event B3: rolling an even number

Set 2

Event A2: rolling a 3 or 5

Event B2: rolling an odd number

Set 4

Event A4: the coin landing heads up

Event B4: the coin landing tails up

10.2: Overtime Wins

Does a hockey team perform differently in games that go into overtime (or shootout) compared to games that don't? The table shows data about the team over 5 years.

year	games played	total wins	overtime or shootout games played	wins in overtime or shootout games
2018	82	46	19	6
2017	82	46	18	7
2016	82	51	23	16
2015	82	54	18	10
2014	82	34	17	5
total	410	231	95	44

Let A represent the event "the hockey team wins a game" and B represent "the game goes to overtime or shootout."

1. Use the data to estimate the probabilities. Explain or show your reasoning.
    a. $P(A)$

    b. $P(B)$

    c. $P(A \text{ and } B)$

    d. $P(A \mid B)$

2. We have seen two ways to check for independence using probability. Use your estimates to check whether each might be true.
    a. $P(A \mid B) = P(A)$

    b. $P(A \text{ and } B) = P(A) \cdot P(B)$

3. Based on these results, do you think the events are independent?

10.3: Genetic Testing

A suspected cause of a disease is a variation in a certain gene. A study gathers at-risk people at random and tests them for the disease as well as for the genetic variation.

	has the disease	does not have the disease
has the genetic variation	80	12
does not have the genetic variation	1,055	1,160

A person from the study is selected at random. Let A represent the event "has the disease" and B represent "has the genetic variation."

1. Use the table to find the probabilities. Show your reasoning.
   a. $P(A)$

   b. $P(B)$

   c. $P(A \text{ and } B)$

   d. $P(A \mid B)$

2. Based on these probabilities, are the events independent? Explain your reasoning.

3. A company that tests for this genetic variation has determined that someone has the variation and wants to inform the person that they may be at risk of developing this disease when they get older. Based on this study, what percentage chance of getting the disease should the company report as an estimate to the person? Explain your reasoning.

Are you ready for more?

Find or collect your own data that can be represented using a two-way table. Some ideas include finding data about a sports team (shooting percentage greater than 50% or less than 50% vs. winning or losing) or clinical trials for a medication (placebo or medication vs. symptom or no symptom).

1. Create a two-way table to represent the sample space.

2. Use probabilities to determine whether events summarized in the table are dependent or independent events.

3. When data is collected in an experiment or a survey it is often difficult to show evidence that events are dependent. Why do you think this occurs? Explain your reasoning.

Lesson 10 Summary

Although it may not always be easy to determine whether events are dependent or independent based on their descriptions alone, there are several ways to check for independence using probabilities.

One way to recognize independence is by understanding the experiment well enough to see if it fits the definition:

- Events A and B are independent if the probability of Event A occurring does not change whether Event B occurs or not.

An example of independence that can be found this way might be the events "a coin landing heads up" and "rolling a 4 on a number cube" when flipping a coin and rolling a standard number cube. Whether the coin lands heads up or not does not change the probability of rolling a 4 on a number cube.

A second way to recognize independence is to use conditional probability:

- Events A and B are independent if $P(A \mid B) = P(A)$

An example of independence that can be found this way might be the events "gets a hit on the second time to bat in a game" and "struck out in the first at bat in a game" for a baseball player in games for a season. By looking at what happens when the player has his second at bat, we can estimate that $P(\text{hit on second at bat}) = 0.324$ and by looking only at the second at bat after a strikeout, we can estimate that $P(\text{hit on second at bat} \mid \text{strike out on first at bat}) = 0.324$ so the events are independent.

Another way to recognize independence is to look at the probability of both events happening:

- Events A and B are independent if $P(A \text{ and } B) = P(A) \cdot P(B)$

An example of independence that can be found this way might be the events "making the first free throw shot" and "making the second free throw shot" for a basketball player shooting two free throws after a foul. By looking at the outcomes of the two shots for the player throughout the year, we can estimate that $P(\text{make the first shot}) = 0.72$, $P(\text{make the second shot}) = 0.72$ and $P(\text{make the first shot and make the second shot}) = 0.52$. The events are independent since $0.72 \cdot 0.72 \approx 0.52$.

Lesson 10 Practice Problems

1. The two-way table shows the number of games played by a team divided into categories based on whether the team warmed up or not as well as whether they made more shots than they missed during the game.

	more shots made	more shots missed
warmed up	14	6
didn't warm up	17	15

One of these games is selected at random. For each question, Event A is "game played when warmed up" and Event B is "more shots made than missed." Use the data to estimate the probabilities.

a. $P(A)$

b. $P(B)$

c. $P(A \text{ and } B)$

d. $P(A \mid B)$

e. Use $P(A \mid B) = P(A)$ and $P(A \text{ and } B) = P(A) \cdot P(B)$ to determine if the two events are dependent or independent. Show or explain your reasoning.

2. The two-way table shows the number of counties in northwestern Iowa where the average corn yield was more than 200 bushels per acre for the years 2016 and 2017.

	2016	2017
more than 200	9	6
200 or less	3	6

a. What does the value 3 represent in the table?

b. What is the probability that a county in northwestern Iowa selected at random had an average corn yield of more than 200 bushels per acre under the condition that it is 2016?

c. For counties in northwestern Iowa, is having an average yield of more than 200 bushels per acre and the year being 2016 or 2017 dependent or independent events? Explain your reasoning.

3. Tyler finds a news article that says, "The price of gasoline has increased to more than $3.00 per gallon and the pay for truck drivers is less than it was last year at this time." Are the events "gasoline costing more than $3.00 per gallon" and "truck driver pay" dependent or independent events? Explain your reasoning.

4. The two-way table summarizes whether or not a cross country team had practice when it was raining and when it was not raining at the end of the school day.

	cross country practice	no cross country practice
raining	6	2
not raining	12	1

a. When it was raining at the end of the school day, what is the probability that cross country practice was held?

b. When it was not raining at the end of the school day, what is the probability that cross country practice was held?

c. Are the events of "holding cross country practice" and "raining at the end of the school day" dependent or independent events? Explain your reasoning.

(From Unit 8, Lesson 9.)

5. Kiran flips a fair coin. If it lands on heads, Kiran will toss the coin again. If it lands on tails, Kiran will roll a standard number cube. What is the probability that Kiran gets heads on his second toss under the condition that he got heads on his first toss?

A. 0

B. 0.25

C. 0.5

D. 1

(From Unit 8, Lesson 8.)

6. Diego randomly selects a card from a standard deck of cards. He places it on his desk and then Clare randomly selects a card from the remaining cards in the same deck.

   a. What is the probability that Diego selects a card that has hearts on it?

   b. What is the probability that Clare selects a card that has hearts on it?

   c. What is the probability that Diego selects a card that has hearts on it and that Clare selects a card that has hearts on it?

   d. Are the events of Diego and Clare randomly selecting a card dependent or independent? Explain your reasoning.

   (From Unit 8, Lesson 7.)

7. A spinner is divided into 8 equal sections. 2 of them are bronze, 1 of them is silver, and 5 of them are gold.

   a. What is the probability that it lands on bronze?

   b. What is the probability that it lands on silver or gold?

   c. What is the probability that it lands on platinum?

   (From Unit 8, Lesson 2.)

Lesson 11: Probabilities in Games

- Let's use probability with games.

11.1: Rock, Paper, Scissors

There is a classic game called "Rock, Paper, Scissors." Two people play by counting to 3 together, then making a hand gesture to resemble paper (hand flat, palm down), rock (fist), or scissors (two fingers extended).

- When paper and rock are shown, paper wins the round.

- When paper and scissors are shown, scissors wins the round.

- When rock and scissors are shown, rock wins the round.

- When both players show the same thing, the round is a tie.

Find a partner and play the game with them 10 times in a row. Record the number of times you have played the game, the name of your opponent, what each person shows in each round, and who is the winner. Find another partner and play another 10 times in a row.

Is the event "win the round" dependent on another event? Explain your reasoning.

Choose an event that you think might influence the probability of winning, then analyze the data using probability to determine whether the event you chose to study is independent of winning. Provide evidence to support your claim.

11.2: Guess Which Card

Your teacher will give you 3 index cards.

- Leave one card blank.

- Use a ruler to draw lines connecting opposite corners to make an X on one side of the second card.

- Use a ruler to draw lines connecting opposite corners to make an X on both sides of the third card.

- Put all three cards in the bag.

One partner will remove a card from the bag and place it on the desk immediately so that only one side of the card can be seen. The goal is to guess correctly which card is on the desk: the blank card, the card with an X only on one side, or the card with an X on both sides.

1. Noah is playing the game and is looking at a card that shows an X. He says, "I have a fifty-fifty chance of correctly guessing which card it is." Do you agree with Noah? Explain your reasoning.

2. Play the game many times with your partner, taking turns for who takes a card out of the bag. Record whether the side that shows has an X or is blank, which card you guess, and which card it actually is when you check. Continue to play until your teacher tells you to move on.

3. Use the results from your games to estimate
   P(the card had an X on both sides | the side showing had an X on it). Explain or show
   your reasoning.

4. Since all of the outcomes are known, find the actual probability
   P(the card had an X on both sides | the side showing had an X on it). Explain or show
   your reasoning.

Lesson 11 Practice Problems

1. The two-way table shows the number of eggs laid by 10 Rhode Island red chickens and 10 leghorn chickens in July and August.

	eggs laid in July	eggs laid in August
Rhode Island red chicken	247	252
leghorn chicken	239	241

A chicken is selected at random. For each question, Event A is "egg laid by a Rhode Island red chicken" and Event B is "egg laid in July." Use the data to estimate the probabilities.

a. $P(A)$

b. $P(B)$

c. $P(A \text{ and } B)$

d. $P(A \mid B)$

e. Use $P(A \mid B = P(A)$ and $P(A \text{ and } B) = P(A) \cdot P(B)$ to determine if the two events are dependent or independent. Show or explain your reasoning.

(From Unit 8, Lesson 10.)

2. Clare finds an article in the online student newspaper that says, "There are more students in the 9th grade this year than last year and there are more students in the 12th grade who are graduating this year than last year." Are the events "the number of students in the 9th grade" and "the number of 12th graders who are graduating" dependent or independent events? Explain your reasoning.

(From Unit 8, Lesson 10.)

3. The two-way table summarizes whether or not a softball team had practice when it was raining and when it was not raining at the start of the day.

	softball practice	no softball practice
raining	4	1
not raining	12	3

a. When it was raining at the start of the day, what is the probability that softball practice was held?

b. When it was not raining at the start of the day, what is the probability that softball practice was held?

c. Are the events of "holding softball practice" and "raining at the start of the day" dependent or independent events? Explain your reasoning.

(From Unit 8, Lesson 9.)

4. Mai rolls a standard number cube and then flips a fair coin. What is the probability that Mai flips heads under the condition that she rolls a 5?

A. $\frac{1}{2}$

B. $\frac{5}{6}$

C. $\frac{1}{12}$

D. $\frac{5}{12}$

(From Unit 8, Lesson 8.)

5. A total of 40 elementary, middle, and high school students participate in a fun run as a fundraiser. They are surveyed after the fun run to find out how many of them completed the fun run without walking. The results of the survey are shown in the table.

	elementary	middle	high
walked during the fun run	8	2	1
did not walk during the fun run	4	14	11

Mai, wants to know the probability that one of the participants in the fun run selected at random is an elementary school student or did not walk during the fun run. To figure this out, she adds the three values in the second row of the table (4, 14, and 11) to the two values listed under the heading "elementary school" (8 and 4). She then divides that answer by 40 and obtains a probability of $\frac{41}{40}$. Mai realizes that $\frac{41}{40}$ is greater than 1 and determines that she must have made a mistake.

a. What is Mai's mistake? Explain your reasoning.

b. How does the addition rule account for this kind of mistake?

(From Unit 8, Lesson 6.)

6. Two classes of middle school students who are going on a field trip were asked if they wanted to go to a science museum or an art museum. Each student selects one museum option. The table summarizes the museum preference of each student in the class.

	science museum	art museum
class A	14	12
class B	11	14

What is the probability that a student in class B selected at random prefers to go to the art museum?

(From Unit 8, Lesson 5.)

7. Elena decides which type of pizza to order. The choices for crust are thin crust, stuffed crust, or regular crust. The choices for one topping are pepperoni, mushrooms, olives, sausage, meatballs, pineapple, or green peppers. Elena has trouble deciding because there are so many possibilities. She selects the type of crust and one topping at random. How many outcomes are in the sample space?

A. 3

B. 7

C. 10

D. 21

(From Unit 8, Lesson 3.)

Learning Targets

Lesson 1: Up to Chance

- I can find or estimate probability using a model or data from a chance experiment.

- I can identify chance experiments.

Lesson 2: Playing with Probability

- I can find the sample space for chance experiments.

- I can model situations using probability.

- I can use sample space to calculate probability.

Lesson 3: Sample Spaces

- I can create organized lists, tables, and tree diagrams and use them to calculate probabilities.

Lesson 4: Tables of Relative Frequencies

- I can use information in a two-way table to find relative frequencies and to estimate probability.

Lesson 5: Combining Events

- I can use tables and Venn diagrams to represent sample spaces and to find probabilities.

Lesson 6: The Addition Rule

- I can use the addition rule to find probabilities.

Lesson 7: Related Events

- I can estimate probabilities, including conditional probabilities, from two-way tables.

Lesson 8: Conditional Probability

- I can estimate probabilities, including conditional probabilities, from two-way tables.

Lesson 9: Using Tables for Conditional Probability

- I can estimate probabilities, including conditional probabilities, from two-way tables.

- I can use probabilities and conditional probabilities to decide if events are independent.

Lesson 10: Using Probability to Determine Whether Events Are Independent

- I can collect data and use it to estimate probabilities.

- I can use probabilities to decide if events are independent.

Glossary

addition rule

The addition rule states that given events A and B, the probability of either A or B is given by $P(\text{A or B}) = P(\text{A}) + P(\text{B}) - P(\text{A and B})$.

altitude

An altitude in a triangle is a line segment from a vertex to the opposite side that is perpendicular to that side.

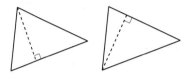

angle bisector

A line through the vertex of an angle that divides it into two equal angles.

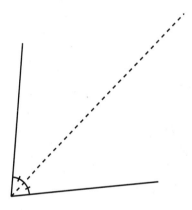

apex

The single point on a cone or pyramid that is the furthest from the base. For a pyramid, the apex is where all the triangular faces meet.

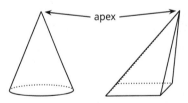

arc

The part of a circle lying between two points on the circle.

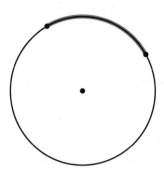

arccosine

The arccosine of a number between 0 and 1 is the acute angle whose cosine is that number.

arcsine

The arcsine of a number between 0 and 1 is the acute angle whose sine is that number.

arctangent

The arctangent of a positive number is the acute angle whose tangent is that number.

assertion

A statement that you think is true but have not yet proved.

auxiliary line

An extra line drawn in a figure to reveal hidden structure.

For example, the line shown in the isosceles triangle is a line of symmetry, and the lines shown in the parallelogram suggest a way of rearranging it into a rectangle.

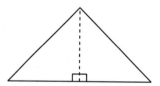
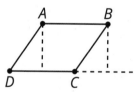

axis of rotation

A line about which a two-dimensional figure is rotated to produce a three-dimensional figure, called a solid of rotation. The dashed line is the axis of rotation for the solid of rotation formed by rotating the green triangle.

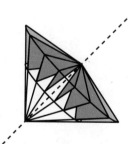

Cavalieri's Principle

If two solids are cut into cross sections by parallel planes, and the corresponding cross sections on each plane always have equal areas, then the two solids have the same volume.

central angle

An angle formed by two rays whose endpoints are the center of a circle.

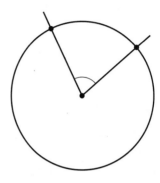

chance experiment

A chance experiment is something you can do over and over again, and you don't know what will happen each time.

For example, each time you spin the spinner, it could land on red, yellow, blue, or green.

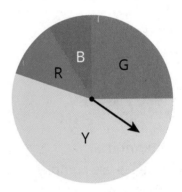

chord

A chord of a circle is a line segment both of whose endpoints are on the circle.

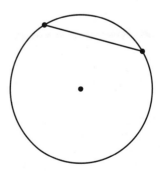

circle

A circle of radius *r* with center O is the set of all points that are a distance *r* units from O.

To draw a circle of radius 3 and center O, use a compass to draw all the points at a distance 3 from O.

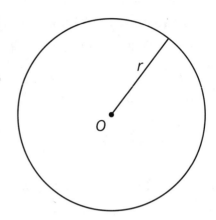

circumcenter

The circumcenter of a triangle is the intersection of all three perpendicular bisectors of the triangle's sides. It is the center of the triangle's circumscribed circle.

circumscribed

We say a polygon is circumscribed by a circle if it fits inside the circle and every vertex of the polygon is on the circle.

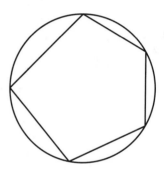

complementary

Two angles are complementary to each other if their measures add up to 90°. The two acute angles in a right triangle are complementary to each other.

conditional probability

The probability that one event occurs under the condition that another event occurs.

cone

A cone is a three-dimensional figure with a circular base and a point not in the plane of the base called the apex. Each point on the base is connected to the apex by a line segment.

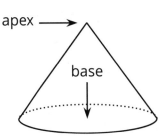

congruent

One figure is called congruent to another figure if there is a sequence of translations, rotations, and reflections that takes the first figure onto the second.

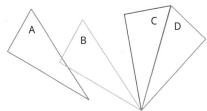

conjecture

A reasonable guess that you are trying to either prove or disprove.

converse

The converse of an if-then statement is the statement that interchanges the hypothesis and the conclusion. For example, the converse of "if it's Tuesday, then this must be Belgium" is "if this is Belgium, then it must be Tuesday."

corresponding

For a rigid transformation that takes one figure onto another, a part of the first figure and its image in the second figure are called corresponding parts. We also talk about corresponding parts when we are trying to prove two figures are congruent and set up a correspondence between the parts to see if the parts are congruent.

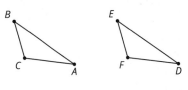

In the figure, segment AB corresponds to segment DE, and angle BCA corresponds to angle EFD.

cosine

The cosine of an acute angle in a right triangle is the ratio (quotient) of the length of the adjacent leg to the length of the hypotenuse. In the diagram, $\cos(x) = \frac{b}{c}$.

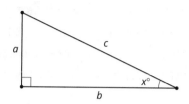

cross section

The figure formed by intersecting a solid with a plane.

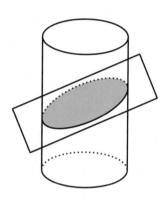 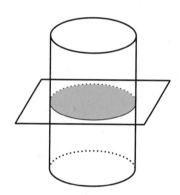 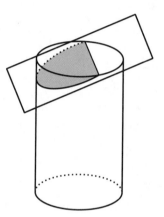

cube root

The cube root of a number x, written $\sqrt[3]{x}$, is the number y whose cube is x. That is, $y^3 = x$.

cyclic quadrilateral

A quadrilateral whose vertices all lie on the same circle.

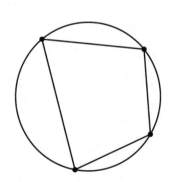

Geometry iM **KH**

cylinder

A cylinder is a three-dimensional figure with two parallel, congruent, circular bases, formed by translating one base to the other. Each pair of corresponding points on the bases is connected by a line segment.

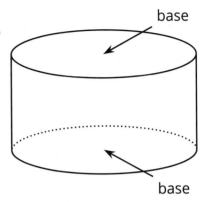

density

The mass of a substance per unit volume.

dependent events

Dependent events are two events from the same experiment for which the probability of one event depends on whether the other event happens.

dilation

A dilation with center P and positive scale factor k takes a point A along the ray PA to another point whose distance is k times farther away from P than A is.

Triangle $A'B'C'$ is the result of applying a dilation with center P and scale factor 3 to triangle ABC.

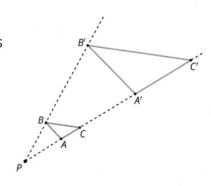

directed line segment

A line segment with an arrow at one end specifying a direction.

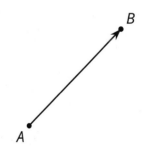

directrix

The line that, together with a point called the focus, defines a parabola, which is the set of points equidistant from the focus and directrix.

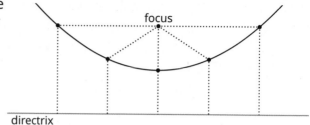

event

An event is a set of one or more outcomes in a chance experiment. For example, if we roll a number cube, there are six possible outcomes.

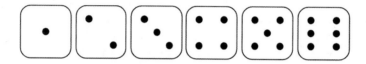

Examples of events are "rolling a number less than 3," "rolling an even number," or "rolling a 5."

face

Any flat surface on a three-dimensional figure is a face.

A cube has 6 faces.

focus

The point that, together with a line called the directrix, defines a parabola, which is the set of points equidistant from the focus and directrix.

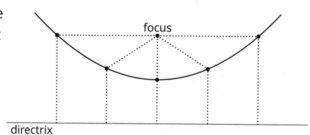

image

If a transformation takes A to A', then A is
the original and A' is the image.

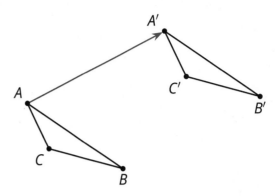

incenter

The incenter of a triangle is the intersection of all three of the triangle's angle bisectors. It
is the center of the triangle's inscribed circle.

independent events

Independent events are two events from the same experiment for which the probability of
one event is not affected by whether the other event occurs or not.

inscribed

We say a polygon is inscribed in a circle if it fits inside the circle and every vertex of the
polygon is on the circle. We say a circle is inscribed in a polygon if it fits inside the polygon
and every side of the polygon is tangent to the circle.

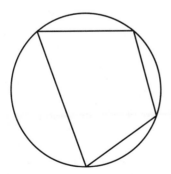 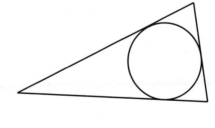

inscribed angle

An angle formed by two chords in a circle that share an endpoint.

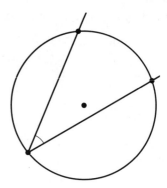

line of symmetry

A line of symmetry for a figure is a line such that reflection across the line takes the figure onto itself.

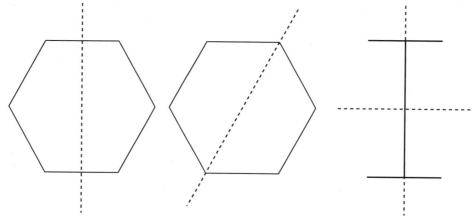

The figure shows two lines of symmetry for a regular hexagon, and two lines of symmetry for the letter I.

line segment

A set of points on a line with two endpoints.

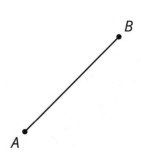

median (geometry)

A line from a vertex of a triangle to the midpoint of the opposite side. Each dashed line in the image is a median.

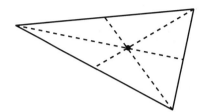

oblique (solid)

Prisms and cylinders are said to be *oblique* if when one base is translated to coincide with the other, the directed line segment that defines the translation is not perpendicular to the bases.

A cone is said to be *oblique* if a line drawn from its apex at a right angle to the plane of its base does not intersect the center of the base. The same definition applies to pyramids whose bases are figures with a center point, such as a square or a regular pentagon.

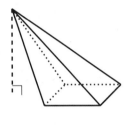
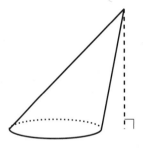

opposite

Two numbers are opposites of each other if they are the same distance from 0 on the number line, but on opposite sides.

The opposite of 3 is -3 and the opposite of -5 is 5.

outcome

An outcome of a chance experiment is one of the things that can happen when you do the experiment. For example, the possible outcomes of tossing a coin are heads and tails.

parabola

A parabola is the set of points that are equidistant from a given point, called the *focus*, and a given line, called the *directrix*.

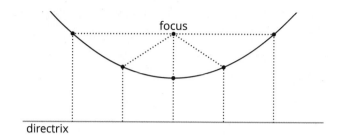

parallel

Two lines that don't intersect are called parallel. We can also call segments parallel if they extend into parallel lines.

parallelogram

A quadrilateral in which pairs of opposite sides are parallel.

perpendicular bisector

The perpendicular bisector of a segment is a line through the midpoint of the segment that is perpendicular to it.

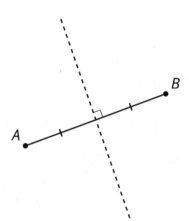

Geometry iM KH

point-slope form

The form of an equation for a line with slope m through the point (h, k). Point-slope form is usually written as $y - k = m(x - h)$. It can also be written as $y = k + m(x - h)$.

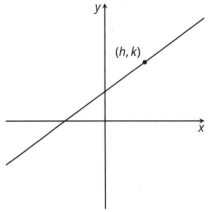

prism

A prism is a solid figure composed of two parallel, congruent faces (called bases) connected by parallelograms. A prism is named for the shape of its bases. For example, if a prism's bases are pentagons, it is called a "pentagonal prism."

rectangular prism   **triangular prism**   **pentagonal prism**

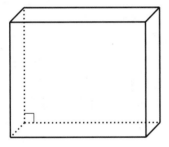 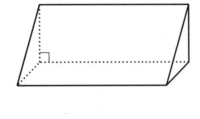 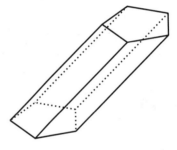

probability

The probability of a chance event is a number from 0 to 1 that expresses the likelihood of the event occurring, with 0 meaning it will never occur and 1 meaning it will always occur.

pyramid

A pyramid is a solid figure that has one special face called the base. All of the other faces are triangles that meet at a single vertex called the apex. A pyramid is named for the shape of its base. For example, if a pyramid's base is a hexagon, it is called a "hexagonal pyramid."

square pyramid

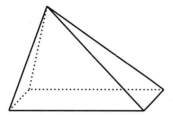

pentagonal pyramid

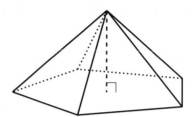

radian

The radian measure of an angle whose vertex is at the center of a circle is the ratio between the length of the arc defined by the angle and the radius of the circle.

reciprocal

If p is a rational number that is not zero, then the reciprocal of p is the number $\frac{1}{p}$.

rectangle

A quadrilateral with four right angles.

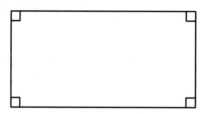

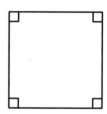

reflection

A reflection is defined using a line. It takes a point to another point that is the same distance from the given line, is on the other side of the given line, and so that the segment from the original point to the image is perpendicular to the given line.

In the figure, A' is the image of A under the reflection across the line m.

Reflect A across line m.

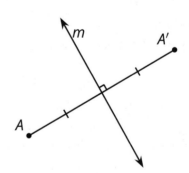

reflection symmetry
A figure has reflection symmetry if there is a reflection that takes the figure to itself.

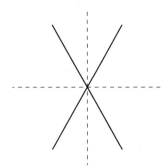

regular polygon
A polygon where all of the sides are congruent and all the angles are congruent.

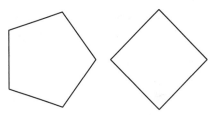

rhombus
A quadrilateral with four congruent sides.

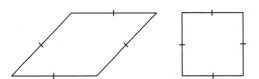

right (solid)
Prisms or cylinders are said to be *right* if when one base is translated to coincide with the other, the directed line segment that defines the translation is perpendicular to the bases.

A cone is said to be *right* if a line drawn from its apex at a right angle to the plane of its base passes through the center of the base. The same definition applies to pyramids whose bases are figures with a center point, such as a square or a regular pentagon.

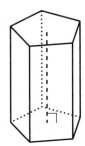 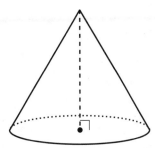 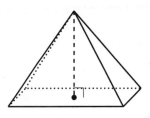

rigid transformation

A rigid transformation is a translation, rotation, or reflection. We sometimes also use the term to refer to a sequence of these.

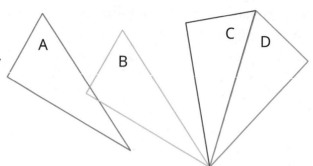

rotation

A rotation has a center and a directed angle. It takes a point to another point on the circle through the original point with the given center. The 2 radii to the original point and the image make the given angle.

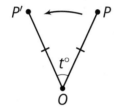

P' is the image of P after a counterclockwise rotation of $t°$ using the point O as the center.

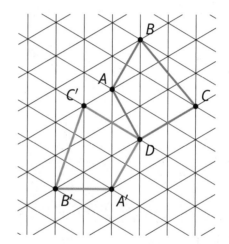

Quadrilateral $ABCD$ is rotated 120 degrees counterclockwise using the point D as the center.

rotation symmetry

A figure has rotation symmetry if there is a rotation that takes the figure onto itself. (We don't count rotations using angles such as 0° and 360° that leave every point on the figure where it is.)

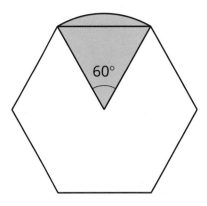

sample space

The sample space is the list of every possible outcome for a chance experiment.

For example, the sample space for tossing two coins is:

heads-heads	tails-heads
heads-tails	tails-tails

scale factor

The factor by which every length in an original figure is increased or decreased when you make a scaled copy. For example, if you draw a copy of a figure in which every length is magnified by 2, then you have a scaled copy with a scale factor of 2.

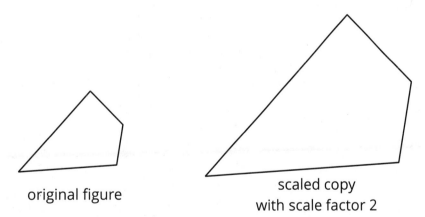

original figure

scaled copy
with scale factor 2

sector

The region inside a circle lying between two radii of the circle.

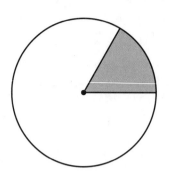

similar

One figure is similar to another if there is a sequence of rigid motions and dilations that takes the first figure onto the second.

Triangle $A'B'C'$ is similar to triangle ABC because a rotation with center B followed by a dilation with center P takes ABC to $A'B'C'$.

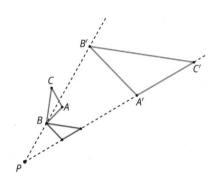

sine

The sine of an acute angle in a right triangle is the ratio (quotient) of the length of the opposite leg to the length of the hypotenuse. In the diagram, $\sin(x) = \frac{a}{c}$.

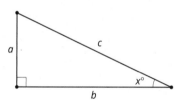

solid of rotation

A three-dimensional figure formed by rotating a two-dimensional figure using a line called the axis of rotation.

The axis of rotation is the dashed line. The green triangle is rotated about the axis of rotation line to form a solid of rotation.

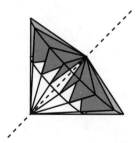

Geometry iM KH

sphere
A sphere is a three-dimensional figure in which all cross-sections in every direction are circles.

symmetry
A figure has symmetry if there is a rigid transformation which takes it onto itself (not counting a transformation that leaves every point where it is).

tangent
The tangent of an acute angle in a right triangle is the ratio (quotient) of the length of the opposite leg to the length of the adjacent leg. In the diagram, $\tan(x) = \frac{a}{b}$.

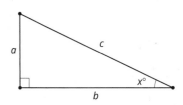

tangent (line)
A line is tangent to a circle if the line intersects the circle at exactly one point.

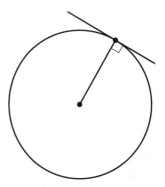

tessellation
An arrangement of figures that covers the entire plane without gaps or overlaps.

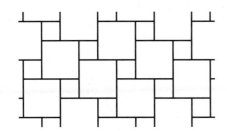
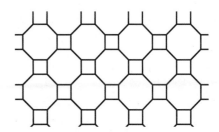

theorem
A statement that has been proved mathematically.

translation

A translation is defined using a directed line segment. It takes a point to another point so that the directed line segment from the original point to the image is parallel to the given line segment and has the same length and direction.

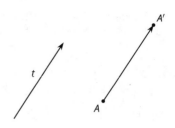

In the figure, A' is the image of A under the translation given by the directed line segment t.

trigonometric ratio

Sine, cosine, and tangent are called trigonometric ratios.

Attributions

"Notice and Wonder" and "I Notice/I Wonder" are trademarks of the National Council of Teachers of Mathematics, reflecting approaches developed by the Math Forum (http://www.nctm.org/mathforum/), and used here with permission.

Images that are not the original work of Illustrative Mathematics are in the public domain or released under a Creative Commons Attribution (CC-BY) license, and include an appropriate citation. Images that are the original work of Illustrative Mathematics do not include such a citation.

Image Attributions

Round Window, by Muntzir. Public Domain. Pixabay. https://pixabay.com/photos/window-house-door-inside-indoors-3065340/.

Bike Wheel, by mohamed_hassan . Public Domain. Pixabay. https://pixabay.com/photos/winter-door-window-wooden-blue-3112188/.

Wagon Wheel, by RoyBuri. Public Domain. Pixabay. https://pixabay.com/photos/dare-wood-wagon-wheel-wheels-2821068/.

Cute Dog, by tatianevasconcelos. Public Domain. Pixabay. https://pixabay.com/photos/dog-pet-animal-canine-mutt-friend-2919014/.

Sparrow on Branch, by gabicuz . Public Domain. Pixabay. https://pixabay.com/photos/sparrow-bird-branch-twig-perched-9950/.

Flying Dog Bat Sleeping, by dustinthewind. Public Domain. https://pixabay.com/photos/flying-dog-zoo-bat-vampire-wing-2623277/.

Coffee Cup, by Free-Photos . Public Domain. Pixabay. https://pixabay.com/photos/coffee-cup-drink-espresso-caffeine-690054/.

Crayons, by Wokandapix . Public Domain. Pixabay. https://pixabay.com/photos/crayons-colors-school-drawing-879974/.

US Nickel, by Lordnikon. Public Domain. Wikimedia Commons. https://commons.wikimedia.org/wiki/File:Usa_one_nickel_1984.JPG.

Citations

Unit 8: Conditional Probability

Lesson 9

Stanford Blood Center https://stanfordbloodcenter.org/donate-blood/blood-donation-facts/blood-types/